Designing in Figma

Eugene Fedorenko

2020

Designing in Figma

by *Eugene Fedorenko*

On the web: *figmabook.com*

Please send errors to *hello@efedorenko.com*

Version 1.1

Copyedited by Doug Warren

To Natalya and Alisa

Contents

Introduction

My first attempt at using Figma was quite disappointing. After scoring an invite to the closed beta in March 2016, I played with it for half an hour. The way it worked in a browser was impressive, but the app was too rough and buggy overall.

A year later, I gave it another try and was thoroughly impressed by the progress the company had made. The whole experience was much more polished. Still, I wasn't ready to use it for my work.

In 2018 Sketch was my primary design tool, but its ecosystem and pay-per-computer pricing became annoying. Essential parts of the workflow, like prototyping, commenting, and handoff, required 3rd-party services, so things became less reliable as there were too many moving parts. My colleague and I split a large design project into multiple smaller files so we could work on them independently without overwriting each other's changes. I also faced issues caused by working on multiple Macs—app versions and plugins were getting out of sync, I had to remember to save and close files before switching to a different computer, and files themselves had to be stored in the cloud.

During all that time, I occasionally used Figma for random illustrations and liked it more and more. Finally, at one point, I imported all my Sketch files with dozens of screens for the current project into Figma and committed to making it work.

Most people starting with Figma fall into one of two camps— they are either switching from Sketch or are entirely new to UI design. This book won't teach you design and focuses only on the app, but where appropriate, I try to discuss fundamentals and best practices. The goal is to help you design efficiently and achieve mastery of the tool.

When switching to Figma in 2018, I looked for a short and concise manual that I could read in a couple of evenings, but all I could find were basic introductions and long video courses. They might work for some, but nothing beats a good manual for me. There is just something special in compressing all the knowledge about the topic or a tool into one book. When done well, the manual can be an elixir of mastery.

To keep the book reasonably short, I focused only on the design process and left prototyping and animations out of scope. They are not as universally used as the design tools, often require external tools or services, and not easy to explain in a written form. I may consider working on these topics separately in the future, but this is still up in the air.

I hope you'll enjoy the book and learn something new from it!

Getting Started

State of Design Tools

For a long time, Photoshop was the primary tool without any serious competition. A few seasoned designers may recall Fireworks as the first tool built for screen design, but personally, I met only a few people who used it in the mid-2000s. Adobe didn't pay much attention to Fireworks after acquiring Macromedia and eventually stopped development after the last release in 2012.

That also was the year when the Sketch app, developed by the Dutch company Bohemian Coding, won an Apple Design Award. While still immature and a little buggy, it felt like a breath of fresh air—the app was specially designed for the needs of UI designers, worked blazingly fast, and felt lightweight. Soon, there was a growing market of apps integrating with it—Craft by InVision for prototyping, Zeplin for developer handoff, Abstract for version control, and a whole lot of plugins addressing different needs.

The beta version of Figma was released in 2015. The company was founded by Dylan Fields and Evan Wallace, who met at Brown University[1]. In 2012 Evan built a WebGL demo with a sphere in a pool of water that immediately made the power of the new technology clear to them[2]. They began with an idea of building a Photoshop-like app in a browser, but soon realized that a mobile app would be a better place for working on photos that primarily were taken on smartphones.

[1] Brown CS Alum Evan Wallace Has Been Named An INC 2019 Rising Star
http://awards.cs.brown.edu/2019/11/11/brown-cs-alums-dylan-field-and-evan-wallace-named-inc-2019-rising-stars/

[2] Interview with CEO of Figma, Dylan Field
https://medium.com/blueprint/interview-with-figma-ceo-dylan-field-d9e05bbd9353

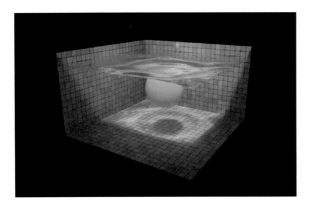

Evan Wallace,
WebGL Water, 2011.
© Figma

After completing several internships at major tech companies, they got frustrated with the lack of cloud-based collaborative tools for interface design and pivoted in this direction. The whole focus on cloud-based technology and interactivity made it a very appealing option both for individual designers and teams looking to improve collaboration.

Today, there is a sizzling competition between Sketch, Adobe XD, Figma, and a few new contenders like InVision Studio and Framer X. All of them are being actively developed, have unique strengths, and provide smart solutions to difficult problems. We can be picky with the options now, but just a few years ago, we would have been happy with any one of them.

Why Switch to Figma?

Comparing apps feature-to-feature is a sure way to make this chapter outdated very soon. (Figma and Sketch ship updates every few weeks, and other competitors are not far behind.) Instead, I'll highlight common reasons among teams switching to Figma.

ENHANCED COLLABORATION

Collaborating in Figma compared to other design tools is like working together in Google Docs compared to editing a Word file in a shared folder. Sure, you can take turns editing and communicate back and forth to avoid overwrites, but the moment you see multiple cursors working together on the same document in real-time, there is no going back. Between collaborating on the same screens with other designers, sharing clickable prototypes with shareholders, and having discussions in comments, there is not much more to wish for.

POWERFUL COMPONENTS

I believe Figma has the most powerful implementation of reusable components. The system of instance overrides is really flexible and includes size, visibility, styles, text, and even nested components. This dramatically reduces the need to detach instances from the main component. All of that will be discussed later in the book.

I also prefer the granular sharing of components from individual documents compared to global Libraries in Sketch. This provides more flexibility when building a design system, improves organization, and reduces the number of components available in every individual document.

BUILT-IN DEVELOPER HANDOFF

Zeplin, Inspect Mode in InVision, Avocode, Sketch Measure plugin—there are tons of 3rd-party tools for passing assets and style-guides from designers to developers, but all of them require maintenance and syncing. Figma's approach is more straight-forward—invite developers to your account with view-only access, and they can reference code snippets and copy assets straight from your original design system. Fewer moving parts is better.

BUILT-IN PROTOTYPING

InVision used to be a go-to app for creating and sharing clickable prototypes, but in 2018 Sketch added their own built-in solution[3]. Still, most people prefer Figma's approach when designs are always in the cloud, and there is nothing to upload before sharing.

3 An in-depth look at Prototyping in Sketch https://blog.sketchapp. com/an-in-depth-look-at-prototyping-in-sketch-942394341f3c

PRICE

Figma's free plan is very generous and probably explains why more than 80% of its active users are currently outside the United States[4]. Being browser-based and free for personal use makes it a fantastic choice for beginners and designers in developing nations, which is uncommon for a high-quality professional app. Most people will need to upgrade only when they ran out of projects, start using it with a team, or decide to build a shareable item library of components.

4 Made in Figma, 2019: Design by the numbers https://www.figma.com/blog/made-in-figma-2019/

Even while the monthly subscription cost for Figma, Sketch, and Adobe XD is in the same ballpark, most teams won't need 3rd-party services like InVision, Zeplin, or Abstract anymore and could significantly reduce the total cost.

MULTI-PLATFORM

As Figma lives in a browser, it works on all major platforms, including Chromebook! Recent updates to iOS and Figurative[5] app make it usable on an iPad as well, but there is no official support yet. This is huge for teams where people may be using multiple platforms and can still collaborate and access files.

5 https://figurative.design

As you may notice, the majority of the reasons to switch are related to Figma's browser-based architecture one way or another. I believe this is a disruptive innovation in action. While other apps are trying to catch up with their cloud-based collaborative tools, most feel like a hack built on top of classic apps. It's similar to tweaking and optimizing a combustion engine, while other manufacturers are shipping electric cars.

Browser vs. Desktop App

Figma's biggest selling point is that it is a browser-based collaborative design tool. It's great that team members don't need to install a new app to review designs, comment, or check values during implementation. But if you're spending significant time in the app, at the very least ensure that your browser is properly configured[6] and install an official Font Installer[7] to make local fonts available in the app.

Better yet, just use their desktop app if you're on macOS or Windows. Here are a few reasons to do this:

- Access to local fonts without running a system service.

- Ability to work in an Unmanaged color space.

- Figma works best in Chrome, but if you primarily use another browser, there is no need to run Chrome just for Figma.

- The app is optimized for and the most stable in the version of Chromium used in the latest desktop app.

- The desktop app preloads editor in the background, so new file creation is much faster.

- More flexibility when exporting assets, as the browser can't save multiple files at once and has to archive them.

- Browser interface doesn't take up valuable screen real estate.

- You can open multiple windows of the app (Shift-Command-N on Mac or Shift-Ctrl-N on Windows). This comes handy when you have multiple displays or working on the same file at different zoom levels.

My only gripe with the desktop app is its two inconsistent menus, one on the system level and anoth-

6 Configure your browser for Figma
https://help.figma.com/hc/en-us/articles/360039828614-Configure-your-browser-for-Figma

7 Figma Downloads
https://www.figma.com/downloads/

er in the app, but this is only a minor annoyance. Besides this, there is no reason to use Figma in the browser, if you can use the app. To make sure that all links to files will open in the right place, enable Preferences → Open Links in Desktop App item in the menu.[8]

If you're feeling brave, Figma provides a beta version of the app with features that haven't been released yet. It may not be stable, but you can try it by downloading from the help article[9].

Figma Interface

Just so we're on the same page when it comes to Figma's interface, let's review it and name its different areas.

On the very top of the Desktop App, a *Tab Bar* provides access to the File Browser (the Figma logo), open documents in tabs, and a button to create a new file. When using Figma in a browser, a Tab Bar is not displayed as only one document can be open in a browser tab.

The *File Browser* shows all your projects and files, which may be viewed in a grid or list view and opened by double-clicking. The plus icons in the Tab Bar and the sidebar create a new draft, while the one in the top-right corner of the File Browser creates a new file in the open project. You can also import a Sketch file using the Import icon in the top-right corner of the File Browser, or File → New from Sketch File... in the "hamburger" dropdown menu.

When viewing a file, there is a *Toolbar* that has a button for opening a "hamburger" menu, a panel of tools, the file name in the center with actions dropdown, and viewing, sharing, and presenting options on the right. The content of the Toolbar changes based on what you have selected on the canvas. A search for menu options can be quickly opened with Command-/ shortcut.

The *Layers* Panel on the left can be toggled with Command-| shortcut. If you have multiple expanded groups or frames, they all can be collapsed with Option-L shortcut. This panel also includes Pages and Assets.

Properties Panel on the right changes based on a current selection and includes Design, Prototype, and Inspect tabs. Both panels and toolbar can be hidden with the Command-\ shortcut, which is convenient if you're working with a large mockup on a small laptop screen.

The main area in the middle of the screen is *Canvas*. Its background color can be changed in the Properties panel. Zoom level can be changed with a few nifty keyboard shortcuts; if you have *Use Number Keys for Opacity* enabled in the Preferences menu, hold Shift to access zooming shortcuts:

- 0 for zooming to 100%
- 1 for fitting all your content on a screen
- 2 for zooming to selection

The shortcut I often use to place selection in the center of the screen is Zoom to Selection (2), followed by Zoom to 100% (0). This can also be achieved by double-clicking on a layer icon in the Layers panel.

Help → Keyboard Shortcuts (or Control-Shift-?) is a great way to learn Figma's keyboard shortcuts. They are nicely organized, and shortcuts you've previously used are shown in blue—this way it's easier to see what you're missing out on. Keep in mind that other apps may have global shortcuts in conflict with Figma. While Figma doesn't allow customizing shortcuts, you can create custom shortcuts on Mac[10] or use 3rd-party apps like Keyboard Maestro[11] for reassigning them.

10 Create keyboard shortcuts for apps on Mac
https://support.apple.com/guide/mac-help/create-keyboard-shortcuts-for-apps-mchlp2271/mac

11 Keyboard Maestro
https://keyboardmaestro.com

Color Space

If you want colors to look consistent across your Figma files, exported images, and browsers, you need to pay attention to color management. It's a vast topic with volumes dedicated to it, so I'll only discuss the bare minimum relevant to Figma.

Every device that can capture or display an image has a color space describing a range of colors that can be represented in an image. sRGB is a default or "least common denominator" standard from 1996 used by a large number of devices and applications. If you have a recent display or laptop, chances are it may have a wider color gamut than sRGB. For example, most devices made by Apple since 2015 have a Display P3 color space, which can show 25% more colors than sRGB.

Figma in the browser is limited to a universal sRGB color space, but the desktop app can be set to use your display's color space by selecting Color Space → Unmanaged in Figma application menu. That puts you into a dangerous situation:

- Colors may appear differently for your team.
- Colors may appear differently between your computers.
- Regardless of your color space, all assets will be exported in the sRGB.
- Every single color format in CSS is in sRGB[12].

12 https://twitter.com/ LeaVerou/status/ 1220030443069878282

While it's exciting to design with the whole spectrum of colors a wide gamut display can show, there is no practical reason to do this until Figma supports color profiles in exports. It can be really disappointing to carefully pick colors in Figma only to see them washed out when exported or applied to the web page. Therefore, make sure that your desktop app's color space is set to sRGB.

Basic Elements

A journey of a thousand miles begins with a single step, while the design of any app starts with basic elements. In this section, we'll review all tools at our disposal in Figma's toolbar and Properties panel. If you think that basic tools like an ellipse or a pen can't be different from any other design app, you'll be surprised.

Move Tools

MOVE TOOL (V)

Move Tool (shortcut V) lets you select, move, and
transform objects. Select one object by clicking on
it, or multiple objects by holding Shift while making
the selection. An object can be excluded from the
selection by clicking one more time while holding
Shift.

You can also select multiple objects by holding the
left mouse button and dragging to create a selection
area containing the objects you want to select. If you
start the selection in the wrong place, you can move
it before the left mouse button is released by holding
the Space bar key.

Hold Command (Ctrl on Windows) while clicking to
select an object nested anywhere inside a group or
frame ("deep select"), or double-click to select an
object one level deeper. We'll talk about navigating
groups and frames in more detail later in the book.

The selected object shows a blue *bounding box* and
dimensions. To measure the distance between the
two objects, select one of them and hold the Option
(Alt on Windows) key while hovering the cursor
over another. The distance will show temporarily
in red. The Option key is also used for duplicating
objects—hold it and drag an object to make a copy.

While the object is selected with the Move Tool, it
can be resized or rotated. Drag a side or a corner
square of the bounding box to resize an object. Hold
the Shift key to constrain proportions while resizing.
Move the cursor slightly outside a corner square
(or press the Command while over it) to rotate the
object.

This is not widely known, but objects can be resized from a keyboard. Select an object and use a combination of Command (Ctrl on Windows) and the arrow keys to change the dimensions one pixel at a time. Hold Shift to change it by 10 pixels, which is a default "big nudge" value that can be changed in Preferences → Nudge Amount. Useful if you need to tweak the size just a little bit.

SCALE TOOL (K)

While it may seem that a separate Scale Tool is excessive, considering the possibilities of the Move Tool, there is a significant difference between them. Move Tool resizes objects while keeping their strokes and effects intact, while Scale Tool will scale them proportionally. It also works for frames, groups, components, instances, and text objects that may be resized but not scaled with Move Tool. We'll talk more about resizing in a chapter on Constraints.

Shape Tools

Figma groups multiple tools for creating basic shapes under the Shape Tools menu in the toolbar. These tools include Rectangle, Ellipse, Line, Arrow, Polygon, Star, and Image.

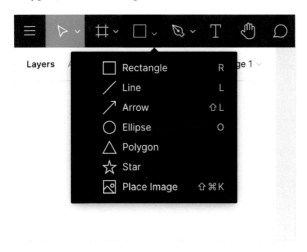

Some of the tools use common modifiers to change their behavior:

- Hold down the Shift key while dragging a cursor to create perfect squares, circles, polygons, and stars.

- Hold down the Option key (Alt on Windows) to create or resize the shape from the center instead of from the corner. This applies to all Shape Tools.

- Shift and Option can be combined to create a shape from the center with all sides of the same length.

- After you press the left mouse button and start dragging a cursor to create a shape, hold the Space bar key to temporarily move the shape without stopping the creation process.

RECTANGLE TOOL (R)

Rectangle Tool is used for recreating rectangles and squares. The keyboard shortcut for the tool is the R key.

Corners can be rounded by specifying a radius in the Inspector section of the Properties panel. The values can be set individually for each corner by clicking on the *Individual Corners* icon. The order of the inputs conveniently matches the shorthand property border-radius in css—top left, top right, bottom right, and bottom left.

Alternatively, you can set a radius with a mouse by hovering over a selected rectangle and moving any of the four circle handles inside it towards the center. To set corner radius individually, hold Option (Alt on Windows) while dragging. If your rectangle already has individually set corner radiuses, holding Option will revert the action and set a unified value.

Corner Smoothing is somewhat buried inside the Individual Corners section. It's an interesting and unique feature shared by multiple tools and will be described in detail at the end of this chapter.

ELLIPSE TOOL (O)

Ellipse Tool (O key) may seem like the dullest tool in the menu until you discover *Arc Tool* used for the creation of additional shapes like pie charts, rings, and broken rings.

After drawing an ellipse or a circle (with the Shift key), hover over it, and a single Arc handle will appear on the right-hand side. By dragging it up or down, you can create a gap in the circle and change the Sweep measured in percentages. When that is done, you'll have three handles—an already familiar Sweep, Start handle controlling where the arc begins, and Ratio handle at the center allowing you to change the circle to the ring.

  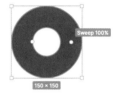

To make a closed ring, you will need first to drag an Arc handle to create a pie, then drag Ratio handle to the desired size for the ring, and finish off by moving the Sweep handle to meet the Start position and close the ring.

LINE TOOL (L)

Line tool (L key) lets you create lines in any direction. You can hold Shift while dragging to create a line at a 45° or 90° angle.

It's better to use a basic Line Tool for drawing simple lines instead of a more powerful Pen Tool because of its adjustable properties. The line created with a Line Tool is recorded as a starting point, length, and angle, while line created with a Pen Tool is recorded as two points in a plane. Any property of the former can be changed later, while the latter can be scaled or rotated only based on its bounding box. It may sound a little confusing, but hopefully, the

illustration and a chapter on Vector Tools will make
it clearer.

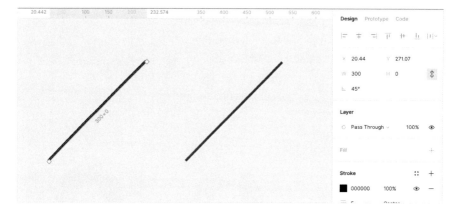

The line created with a Line Tool is recorded as 300
pixels long at 45 degrees.

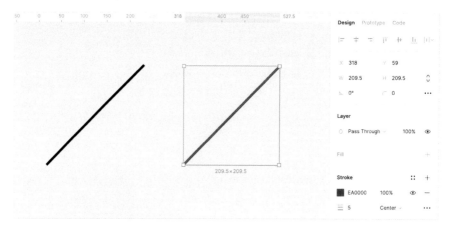

The line created with a Pen Tool is recorded as a
square object with two connected points. The object
can be scaled or rotated, but the line's properties
like angle or length can't be changed directly.

ARROW TOOL (SHIFT-L)

The tool that shouldn't exist and probably was
added only to bring visibility to the feature. It's
pretty simple—you create a line, and its endpoint is
displayed as an arrow. The arrow's size depends on

a stroke width, which can be inconvenient if you're looking to create a thin but large arrow.

Why shouldn't it exist? Any line created with a Line Tool or Pen can be converted into a line with an arrow in *Advanced Stroke* properties. If you pick Line Arrow or Triangle Arrow as a Cap, both ends will be turned into arrows. If only one endpoint should have an arrow, you'll need to select a line, click Edit Object button in context toolbar, select the point, and then pick its Cap. This way, you can even create a line with two different arrows on the ends.

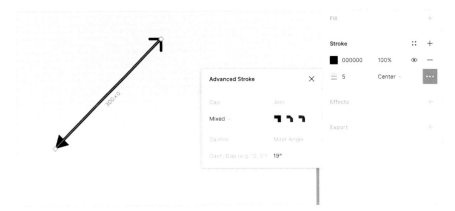

POLYGON

Polygons can have any number of sides between 3 and 60. The count can be changed either in the Inspector or by selecting a polygon, then dragging a circle handle on one of the corners.

The bounding box of a polygon extends beyond the shape itself to keep the size consistent when the number of sides is changed. It can be snapped to the shape's true boundary by flattening (either right-click on the polygon and select Flatten or press Command-E on Mac or Ctrl-E on Windows). Keep in mind that at this moment, the polygon converts into a vector shape, and the number of sides can't be changed anymore.

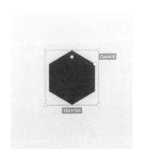

A single value for the corner radius can be set either by entering it into the Inspector field or dragging a circle handle inside a polygon. At first glance, it appears that setting an individual corner radius is not supported, but in editing mode, it can be set for any number of selected points. (Hold Shift to select multiple points.) Editing mode for any vector shape can be entered by double-clicking on an object, pressing the Return on the keyboard, or clicking Edit Object in the toolbar.

STAR

Properties of the Star Tool are very similar to the Polygon Tool, because technically star is a type of non-convex polygon[1]. There are two primary differences:

1 Star polygon
https://en.wikipedia.org/wiki/Star_polygon

1. Stars are defined by a number of points instead of sides, so a default 5-pointed star has 10 sides.

2. The Ratio is the distance of the inner points of the star from the center. It's defined as a percentage of the star's overall diameter.

Just as in polygons, corner radius can be set as a unified value for the shape or individually for each corner.

PLACE IMAGE (SHIFT-COMMAND-K)

It may not be obvious what images have to do with the Shape Tools menu until we see how they are implemented in Figma. Both vector and raster images can be placed, but they work differently.

Vector images placed from SVG become a new frame with fully editable vector shapes. If you're into web development, there is a neat trick for copying SVG from an editor or a web page straight to Figma. In an editor or a browser's Inspector, select an SVG code and copy it to the clipboard. Now it can be pasted straight to Figma without saving to a file.

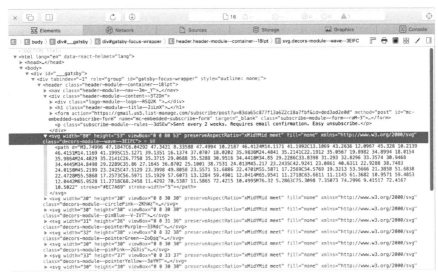

SVG code in a browser's Inspector.

Raster images (PNG, JPEG, GIF, TIFF, and WEBP) are supported as one of the types of the shape's Fill. When you place a raster image, a rectangle shape matching the image's original size is created, and the image is applied as its Image Fill. This implementation provides the flexibility of dragging an image file on top of any shape's Fill section to create a custom-shaped illustration. That explains why Place Image is part of the Shape Tools menu.

One common problem is that by default, raster images are placed in their non-retina size. This is easy to fix thanks to Figma's smart input fields. Make sure that Constrain Properties is enabled and use width or height field as a calculator. For example, if the original width was 250, change it to 250/2 and press Return. Both properties will recalculate automatically. Alternatively, you can enter 50% or any other percentage value. Other math operations are supported as well, so experiment with them!

If you need less precision, *scrubbing* a numeric field can be worth trying. Try hovering over a field label until the cursor changes to an arrow, then click and move it to increase or decrease the value.

WHAT IS CORNER SMOOTHING?

Back in 2013, Apple released iOS 7, where square app icons with rounded corners were replaced with *squircles*. To an untrained eye, they may look the same, but squircles have a much smoother curvature, like if a regular rounded corner was finished with sandpaper to smooth over the part where the rounding begins. The shape looks more natural, resembling a river pebble or a half-used bar of soap. Unsurprisingly, they are pretty common in industrial designers—just look at smooth corners of a MacBook or an iPhone.

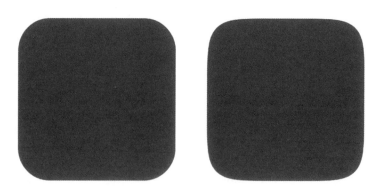

Regular rounded corners vs. squircles

Figma wanted to meet the needs of designers looking to use squircles in their projects. They couldn't just smooth over all rounded corners, as that would make any implementation on the web using border-radius css property look too different from a design mockup. Instead, they added a *Corner Smoothing* slider that softly changes curvature from a regular rounded corner to squircles, with a special mark at 60% that closely matches iOS style.

Generally speaking, it's better not to use Corner Smoothing for web projects at all, set it to iOS mark for projects designed for that platform, and use maximum smoothing in illustrations and icons that will be exported as an image. If you want to learn more about squircles, check out Figma's very detailed and math-heavy blog post "Desperately seeking squircles"[2].

2 https://www.figma.com/ blog/desperately-seeking-squircles/

BLOBS

Sometimes standard shapes aren't enough, and that's where plugins help. *Blobs* by Dylan Feltus creates unique blob shapes based on the specified complexity of the shape. Pretty cool and versatile.

Blobs

Generate random blobs in your designs

Customize complexity & contrast
Smooth and crisp vectors
Unique every time

Vector Editing Toolset

When Figma founders set to build the Pen Tool without a prior design background, they got surprised at how unintuitive it was in other apps [3]. Some of the limitations were dragged from the early days of design tools and didn't really make sense anymore. They rethought the tool from the ground up and came up with one of the most unique parts of Figma— *Vector Networks*. At first glance, vector editing in Figma works just as in all other apps, but the extra powers are just sitting there waiting to be discovered.

3 Introducing Vector Networks

https://medium.com/figma-design/introducing-vector-networks-3b877d2b864f

PEN TOOL

A Vector Network consists of paths. Each path is a chain of linked lines and curves from one endpoint to the other. Lines are defined by starting and ending points, while Bézier curves have additional control points to define their curvature. In most drawing tools, each point can have either one or two paths coming off it. In Figma, **any number of paths can come off one point.** That reduces the number of individual objects and allows much faster creation of complex shapes within the same object and with the same properties.

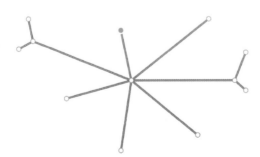

A single vector network object.

The Pen is the primary tool for working with vector networks in Figma. Every click creates a new point connected to the path with the straight line. To curve a line, click and drag the control point of a Bézier curve out of the point. To continue from a different point, press Esc to drop the connection, select an existing point or add a new one, and continue building a path from it.

While working on a path, you can temporarily access extra tools by pressing modifier keys. Clicking on any point with Option (Alt on Windows) will remove it. Holding Shift will help create a line at 45° or 90° angles. (There is also a red line showing up automatically whenever your cursor is on the same line as another point.) Holding Command (Ctrl on Windows) turns on a Bend Tool.

PENCIL TOOL (SHIFT-P)

The Pencil is a tool for freeform drawing—you hold the button down and draw, while all the points and curves are created automatically. The resulting path can be edited later in vector editing mode. Pencil can be useful while working on illustrations, but in general, it's less precise than Pen Tool.

Having Wacom or another pen tablet on hand makes it more useful. If you have an iPad and Apple Pencil, the Figurative app makes Figma entirely usable on it even without official support. Whatever tool you use, I recommend installing *Pencil Pal* plugin that lets you choose both fill and stroke before drawing with a pen.

VECTOR EDITING MODE

As you might have noticed, while using the Pen Tool, the app enters vector editing mode and the standard toolbar is replaced with an editing toolbar. This

mode is used for editing any vector object created with Drawing Tools, Shape Tools, or placed from an external vector file. To enter it, select an object and double-click it, or press the Return key, or click Edit Object button in the toolbar.

While in Vector Editing mode, you can select a point and hold the Option key (Alt on Windows) to see the distance to other points on hover. Precise measurements between points work exactly the same as measurements between objects.

BÉZIER CURVES

Bézier curves were first invented over half a century ago for designing the bodywork of French cars. In modern vector design tools, they are used for creating precisely controlled, scalable, and smooth curves that can be combined into paths. They are also used in animations and motion graphics, but this is off-topic. There are different types, but vector tools in general and Figma in particular use *cubic Bézier curves*.

Bézier curves are manipulated by handles [4] that extend from the endpoints. At the end of each handle is the control point. By moving the control point, the shape of the curve can be changed.

4 The Bézier Game is a good way to learn theory through practice.

https://bezier.method.ac

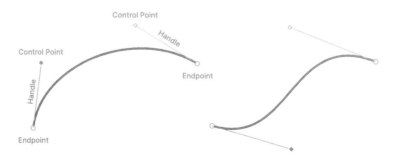

The curve starts at the endpoint and gets (almost magnetically) attracted to the handle control point coming out of it. It ends at the second endpoint, attracted to its own control point. The length of handles and their direction determines how far and how sharply the curve bends.

Paths with Multiple Points

We covered a single curve between the two points, but most paths consist of multiple points. As such, if point connects two curves into a single path, there may be two handles extending from it—one for each curve. Let's go through all possible scenarios.

The point connecting two straight lines will have **no handles** because there are no Bézier curves in this path.

If one of the lines is turned into a Bézier curve (let's say with Bend Tool), there will be **only one handle** coming out of the connecting endpoint to control the curvy part of the path.

If both parts of the path consist of curves, the connecting endpoint will have **two handles** to control parts of both curves.

Handles Mirroring

The last case with two handles on the endpoint is worth pausing at. The two handles can have different types of relationships that will form various curves and angles—from sharp-angled to silky-smooth. Select the endpoint, and you can see a drop-down with mirroring options in the Vector section of Properties panel.

No Mirroring sets both handles acting completely independently of each other. This is the best option if you want to create an obvious angle or corner in your path. Alternatively, this option is handy if you want to get rid of one of the handles—select the control point and press the Delete key.

Mirror Angle is used for building a smooth Bézier curve without a visible angle, as in the previous option. The handles are placed at 180° to each other and form a single line but can have a different length. This is useful when the curve needs to taper off differently on one of the sides.

Mirror Angle and Length is the best method for building a completely smooth Bézier curve. Not only are both handles at the same angle, but they also have the same length. If you were creating an ellipsis or a sine wave with a Bézier curve, that would be the right tool for the job.

Best Practices

- Try to reduce the number of points in your path to a minimum. The fewer points there are, the smoother the path will be.

- Place endpoint on the outermost point of the curve instead of stretching it with handles.

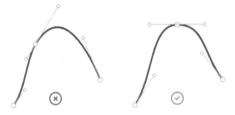

- One common approach is to place handles only horizontally or vertically with the Shift key pressed. It works best in combination with the previous recommendation. Not a universal rule, but limiting the number of variables in the process usually increases work speed.

DIRECT MANIPULATION AND BENDING

Direct manipulation of paths and vector networks is possible as an alternative to precise adjustments by moving points and adjusting control handles. Any section of the path can be selected and dragged around in edit mode, and all connected paths will be moved accordingly.

There is also a **Bend Tool** (to which you can switch temporarily with Command or Ctrl shortcut key) that manipulates the curve directly without touching individual control points.

COLOR FILL

Figma's move from the familiar concept of enclosed paths to vector networks put their tools for **filling areas with color** on steroids as well. It starts by automatically filling all enclosed space, but provides **Paint Bucket** (B) tool for granular control over which sections should or shouldn't be filled.

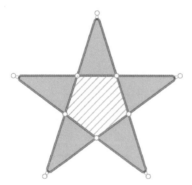

CORNER RADIUS

Another nice touch is that Corner Radius (and even Corner Smoothing!) is available for vector networks and custom shapes. Rounding gets applied only to corners between two lines at straight endpoints without handles. An individual value can be set for every corner in edit mode. Behind the scenes, Figma creates its own set of Bézier curves for a rounded corner. To make them visible and editable, you can *Flatten* the path, which will be covered in the next chapter.

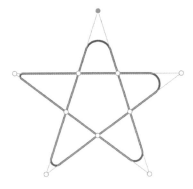

Boolean Groups

Shape Tools and the vector editing toolset provide a powerful way to create shapes, but sometimes they are not enough. That's when Boolean Group operations come into play and offer multiple ways to unite or subtract shapes. They require two or more layers and produce a special boolean group with resulting shape and shared fill and stroke properties.

The operations are in the Boolean Groups dropdown in the contextual part of the toolbar. It appears only when more than one shape is selected.

There are four Boolean Groups operations:

- **Union** combines the selected shapes. The overlapping shapes will be combined into a shape based on all shapes' outer path and excluding all the segments that overlap.

- **Subtract** is the opposite of the Union. The overlapping shapes will be cut out from the shape in the *bottom* selected layer.

- **Intersect** creates a boolean group whose shape consists only of the overlapping segments of the selected shapes.

- **Exclude** is the opposite of Intersect and creates a shape only from the segments that do not overlap (as if you *subtracted* the Intersect shape from the Union shape.)

Union   Subtract   Intersect   Exclude

Union and Subtract operations get used the most, although Intersect and Exclude can be occasionally useful as well. Subtract is the only one where the order of the layers matters. All the operations are non-destructive, so the boolean group can be un-grouped later, and participating shapes can be edited or moved as long as the group wasn't *flattened*.

FLATTEN SELECTION (COMMAND-E)

Flattening converts the selection into a single vector shape, while destroying information about individual shapes, boolean groups, and rounded corners. It may sound undesirable, but there are a few valid reasons to want this:

- After applying a Boolean Group operation to shapes, you may want to manually edit intersection points or Bézier curves on a resulting path.

- Before exporting the shape into svg, you may flatten it to delete a few extraneous vector points and reduce file size.

- If you're going to rotate the shape, but don't want its directional styling to be rotated as well. As an example, think of linear gradients or drop shadows.

- The bounding box of a Polygon or Star extends beyond the shape itself and affects the alignment of elements.

Flattening is a highly destructive action, so it's worth keeping in mind two things:

- Rounded corners will be converted to Bézier curves. Sometimes it's a good idea to flattened the shape before applying rounded corners to it.

- Backup your work! Duplicate and hide layers you are going to flatten, just in case you'll need to come back to them later.

Masks

An outline mask, also known as a *clipping mask*, is a shape that only reveals content within its boundaries. It's similar to looking through a cutout on a sheet of paper—there are lots to see around, but your view is limited to the shape of the cutout. If you move your cutout (or mask), a different part of the view will be revealed.

Two masks reveal different parts of the same group of shapes.

Any shape, group, or boolean group can be turned into a mask by clicking "Use as Mask" (Control-Command-M) button in the toolbar, or right-clicking on the layer and selecting the same command from the context menu. A new group with a masked shape will be created. The mask will apply to all layers above it in that group.

In addition to outline masks, Figma also supports **alpha masks** in imported raster images. Only PNG may have an alpha channel, so it's the only supported format. Unlike outline masks that use shape, alpha masks use the per-pixel opacity of the raster image. This creates some cool possibilities, like masking an image with a gradient.

Alpha mask.

Keep in mind that raster images are not as scalable as vectors, so if enlarged, they could have visible artifacts. On this image, it's easy to tell the difference between vector shapes and an alpha mask boundary.

Raster artifacts.

Fill, Stroke, and Effects

Objects can be filled with colors and gradients, outlined with strokes, and decorated with various effects. Let's give the options a close look.

FILL

By default, objects are filled with an opaque solid color, but can have multiple fills of different paint types—solid colors, gradients, and images. Every fill is treated as a separate layer and may have its own transparency level and blend mode. Default fill and stroke can be changed by selecting a layer with the desired styles and applying Edit → Set Default Properties.

Solid Colors and Color Models

Solid fills are defined by one of five color models:

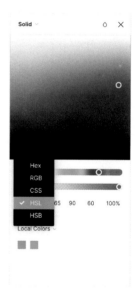

- **RGB**—Red, Green, and Blue values (0–255) are used by a computer to display colors. It's not very human-friendly, but all other color models are based on it.

- **Hex**—hexadecimal representation of the RGB value, commonly used in web design and software development. It's quite universal and easy to copy and paste as a single value, but also hard to adjust manually.

- **CSS**—decimal representation of the RGB value with an Alpha channel for the opacity (from fully transparent at 0 to completely opaque at 1) in one of the CSS formats. Easy to copy and paste while working on a web project.

- **HSL**—Hue, Saturation, and Lightness (or Luminance) is an alternative representation of the RGB color model based on the way human vision perceives colors. *Hue* reflects a pure color on a color wheel (from 0° to 360°), *Saturation* shows the richness of color (from the palest grey at 0 to the richest at 100), and *Lightness* goes from the darkest black at 0 to the brightest white at 100.

- **HSB**—Hue, Saturation, and Brightness (also known as HSV) is similar to HSL, with the difference in how Saturation and Brightness are calculated. 100% Brightness in HSB will produce the white color only when the Saturation is 0, while in HSL, 100% Lightness will always produce the white color regardless of the Saturation.

HSL and HSB are the best models for design work and granular control—they are indispensable for adjusting brightness and saturation of a base color[5]. Hex, CSS, or RGB models are great for referencing colors during implementation. Switch between them based on the kind of work you're doing at the moment. Keep in mind that these color models are used only for representing colors while working in Figma. During export, all values will be converted to the sRGB color profile.

You can use one- or three-character shortcuts when entering color values in Hex format. A single character will be replicated to all six characters and handy for quickly entering shades of grey, like 3 for 333333, or A for AAAAAA. Three character shortcuts work just as in CSS, where 63C becomes 6633CC.

The **eyedropper tool** inside the Color Picker lets you sample a solid color from any object or image in a file. It can be invoked by the keyboard shortcut i when you have the Color Picker open. When closed, the same shortcut (or its alternative Ctrl-C) will replace the topmost fill with the selected color.

It's important to keep accessibility in mind when selecting colors for your project. Web Content Accessibility Guidelines (WCAG) recommend specific contrast ratios for small and large text, as well as

5 See also on HSL and HSB:

RGB vs HSB vs HSL—Demystified

https://medium.com/innovaccer-tech/rgb-vs-hsb-vs-hsl-demystified-1992d7273d3a

HSL and HSV

https://en.wikipedia.org/wiki/HSL_and_HSV

images. Plugin *Contrast* makes it extremely easy to scan your project for contrast issues or check individual combinations. There are multiple choices for accessibility plugins, but this one is free and, in my opinion, works the best.

Gradients

In addition to the solid colors, Figma also provides four types of **gradients**—Linear, Radial, Angular, and Diamond. All of them progressively blend colors and/or transparency from the start to end point using one of these techniques:

- Linear gradient transitions in a straight line.
- Radial gradient spreads out from the center.
- Angular gradient sweeps clockwise from the starting point.
- Diamond gradient creates a diamond shape.

| Linear | Radial | Angular | Diamond |

Gradients are defined by a color combination, just as much as by their type. There are a few common schemes worth considering:

- Adding a soft *monochromatic* gradient to solid colors may not be in line with a flat design trend, but it makes everything look more natural and brings depth and dimension to the design. In real life, colors are never completely flat and always have highlights and shadows from the surrounding light sources. It's a good idea to figure out where

your light is coming from and keep the source consistent across all elements.

- *Analogous* colors are next to each other on the color wheel and can produce beautiful and natural-looking gradients. To create them, keep the Hue difference within 60–120°.

- Gradients between a pair of *complimentary* colors (direct opposites on a color wheel with a difference in Hue of 180°) often look muddy because color travels across the spectrum through the point of no saturation. Changing Hue difference to 160–200° can help, but they can also be improved by adding an extra point to shift the direction of the transition.

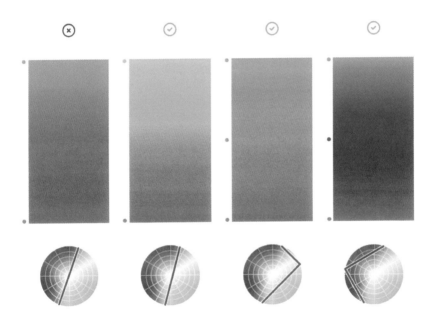

- If you're looking for a smooth transition without a sharp line at the starting point of an angular gradient, try moving the start and end points apart or having more than two points.

- Adobe Color[6] and uiGradients[7] are great resources for exploring color combinations. Another infinite source of color inspiration is nature—look for photos with a color scheme you have in mind and pick colors from it with an eyedropper tool.[8]

- *Webgradients* plugin includes a collection of beautiful and easy-to-use gradients.

6 https://color.adobe.com

7 https://uigradients.com

8 The Secret of Great Gradient
https://uxplanet.org/the-secret-of-great-gradient-2f2c49ef3968

Image Fill

I mentioned this type of fill while describing Place Image in Shape Tools. Any shape can be filled with a raster image in one of four ways:

- *Fill* covers the whole shape with the image.

- *Fit* shows as much of the image as possible within a given shape.

- *Crop* scales the shape without affecting proportions of the image. This is a default mode when using the Place Image button in the toolbar. You can crop an object with any Image Fill by double-clicking on it while holding Option or Alt key.

- *Tile* repeats the image within the shape and provides a way to adjust the size of every tile.

You can insert multiple images into shapes at once.
Select Place Image tool in the toolbar or press
Shift-Command-K, and select multiple images from
the disk. Your cursor will turn into a stack of images
with a red counter, and now you can click on objects
one by one to apply them as Image fills.

Figma also provides a simple built-in raster editor
with basic controls like rotation, exposure, contrast, saturation, temperature, tint, highlights, and
shadows. The following formats are supported: PNG,
JPEG, GIF, TIFF, and WEBP. Due to browser limitations,
the width and height of an image must not be larger
than 4096 pixels.

It may be unexpected, but Figma also supports animated GIFs. The animation is not shown in the editor (although you can pick a frame to display), but
can be viewed in Presentation View. This is a great
way to add realistic spinners, subtle animations, and
video elements to your prototypes. It shows as a GIF
in the list to differentiate from regular Image fills
and can be played in the Image Adjustments panel. [9]

9 Bring Figma prototypes to
life with GIFs

https://www.figma.com/blog/
bring-figma-prototypes-to-
life-with-gifs/

Used image as a fill, but now want to export it from
Figma in the original resolution? That will require a
little hack. Select an object with an Image fill, go to
the Inspect tab in the Properties panel, then switch
it to Table view. Click a blue file name, and it'll open
the original file in a new browser window.

Multiple Fills

Layers can have more than one fill placed on top of
each other. They can be reordered by dragging an
icon that appears on hover on the left side of the fill.
Fills can also be temporarily hidden by clicking on
the eye icon, or removed by clicking on the minus
icon.

Blend Modes

Blending modes determine how colors of objects blend with the colors of underlying objects and can be applied to individual fills, layers, and groups. They are pretty standard across design tools and easy to play with, but fully understanding how they work can help with achieving desired effects[10].

It's best to discuss blending modes in terms of color terminology:

- The *blend color* is the original color of the selected layer or fill.
- The *base color* is the underlying color.
- The *resulting color* is what's produced by blending them together.

Figma provides the following conveniently grouped modes.

- **Normal** is the default blend mode that fills the object with the *blend color* without interaction with the *base color*. If the color has transparency, the process called *alpha compositing* is applied to create a combination of two colors.

10 Extra reading on blending modes:

PDF Blend Modes

https://www.adobe.com/content/dam/acom/en/devnet/pdf/pdfs/pdf_reference_archives/blend_modes.pdf

Blending Modes Explained — The Complete Guide to Photoshop Blend Modes

https://photoshoptrainingchannel.com/blending-modes-explained/

The Ultimate Visual Guide to Understanding Blend Modes

https://www.slrlounge.com/workshop/the-ultimate-visual-guide-to-understanding-blend-modes/

About blending modes

https://helpx.adobe.com/illustrator/using/transparency-blending-modes.html#about_blending_modes

Blend modes for darkening colors:

- **Darken** selects the darkest values in RGB channels of the blend and base colors as the resulting color. Base colors lighter than the blend color are replaced, and those darker than the blend color do not change.

- **Multiply** mode multiplies the RGB channel values from the blend color with the base color's values. The result is always a darker color. Multiplying any color with black produces black (as multiplying by zero), and with white leaves the color unchanged (as multiplying by one). The visual effect is similar to drawing with multiple markers on top of each other.

- **Color Burn** darkens the base color to reflect the blend color. The darker the base color, the more its color is used. Blending with white color produces no difference. When blend color is homogeneous, this effect is equivalent to changing the black point of the base color.

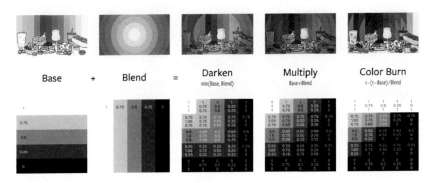

Blend modes for darkening colors.
Table illustration by by Elsma Ramirez, blush.design.

Blend modes for lightening colors:

- **Lighten** selects the lightest values in RGB channels of the blend and base colors as the resulting color. Base colors darker than the blend color are replaced, and ones lighter than the blend color do not change.

- **Screen** mode has the opposite effect to Multiply. It multiplies the inverse RGB channel values of the blend and base colors, so the result is always lighter. The effect is similar to projecting multiple images to a single screen.

- **Color Dodge** lightens the base color to reflect the blend color. The lighter the base color, the more its color is used. Blending with black color produces no change. When blend color is homogeneous, this effect is equivalent to changing the white point of the base color.

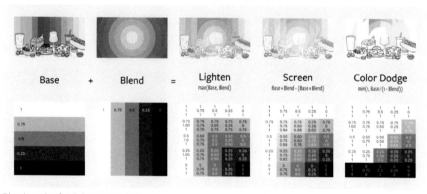

Blend modes for lightening colors.

The combination of above blend modes for changing contrast:

- **Overlay** is a combination of Multiply and Screen modes, depending on the base color value. Blend colors overlay the base color, while preserving its highlights and shadows. The base color is not replaced, but mixed with the blend color to reflect the lightness or darkness of the base.

- **Soft Light** darkens or lightens the colors, depending on the blend color value. The effect is similar to shining a diffused spotlight on the base.

- **Hard Light** is a combination of Multiply and Screen modes, but unlike Overlay, it depends on the blend color value. The effect is similar to shining a harsh spotlight on the base.

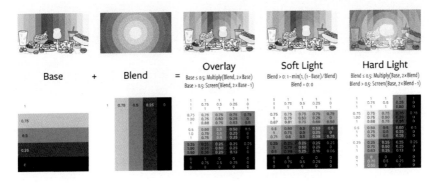

The combination of darkening and lightening modes.

Arithmetic blend modes can produce interesting effects:

- **Difference** subtracts the darker of the two colors from the lighter. Blending with black produces no change, while blending with white inverts the base color. Can be used to verify the alignment of objects with similar content.

- **Exclusion** is a lower contrast variation of Difference mode.

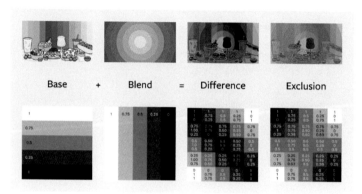

Arithmetic modes.

Blend modes based on an HSL color model:

- **Hue** applies hue of the blend color to the base color.

- **Saturation** applies saturation of the blend color to the base color.

- **Color** applies both hue and saturation of the blend color to the base color. Useful for tinting images to a specific color.

- **Luminosity** applies luminosity of the blend color to the base color.

HSL-based modes.

In raster image editors like Photoshop, blend modes can be used to manipulate the exposure of specific areas with Dodging and Burning, increase sharpness with Luminosity, or contrast with Overlay. But what can they be used for in Figma and other vector editors?

Besides the obvious application in illustrations, blend modes can be used in UI design for quickly tweaking color scheme with HSL modes, applying specific tint with Color, or adjusting overall exposure and contrast. Consider using them for quick experiments, especially in combination with Masks to limit the area of application.

While working on a dark mode of the *People-First Jobs* website, an unexpected use case for blend modes came up. The original logo was designed to be used on a light background, and colors of overlapping sections were blended in Multiply mode.

The effect is similar to drawing the logo with three markers when overlapping sections become darker. That didn't look right on a dark background.

Knowing that Screen blend mode is the opposite of Multiply, I set colors of overlapping sections with it for the dark mode. That produced a version that looked much better on a dark background, but still was consistent with the original logo.

Layer Opacity vs. Color Opacity

You might have noticed that both colors and layers have a way to set a blend mode and opacity. They should be set for the whole layer when you want an object to have a consistent blending and level of transparency. Color opacity can be applied more selectively. Besides, opacity is saved along with the color in Styles, so if you want to change the opacity

of an object filled with a Color Style, changing a layer's opacity may be the only way.

You can choose to use number keys for setting a layer opacity in Preferences → Use Number Keys for Opacity under the hamburger menu. That will overwrite a standard behavior of using number keys for zooming—1 to zoom to fit, 2 to zoom to selection, and 0 to zoom at 100%.

STROKE

Strokes are defined by their fills, width, alignment, and a few advanced properties. We already covered fills in a previous section, width is quite self-explanatory, and alignment defines if the stroke will be drawn inside, outside, or at the center of the path. Advanced settings are a little more interesting.

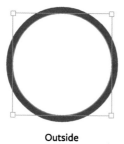  

Outside   Center   Inside

I mentioned **Cap** before when discussing the Arrow Tool. Cap provides a way to make an endpoint on an open path rounded, square, or to decorate it with one of two arrow styles. A unique Cap style can be picked for any endpoint on a path.

Join styles define what connections between parts of a path look like—Miter, Bevel, or Round. Surprisingly, terminology for both Miter and Bevel comes from woodworking. Small **Miter Angle** results in a sharp joint, and as it increases, it becomes the same as Bevel.

Dashed strokes can be based on as few as two com-ma-separated values—widths of dash and gap—and as many as 8 for more complicated designs.

EFFECTS

Objects can have four kinds of effects applied to them—Inner Shadow, Drop Shadow, Layer Blur, and Background Blur. (In case you're designing for the web, all of them have matching css properties.) While blurs can be applied only once, up to eight shadows of every kind can be stacked together for tight control over the result. Effects take their toll on Figma performance, so if you experience slowness, try to use blurs sparingly and reduce the number of stacked shadows.

In the real world, shadows depend on the position and intensity of light sources. In user interfaces, light is usually coming from the front (iOS), front-top (macOS), or top-left corner (Classic Mac OS and Windows 95). It's best to keep light sources and resulting shadows consistent with screens you're working on and environment you're designing for (OS, browser chrome, etc.) Shadow's position can be controlled with X and Y offset, and intensity with Blur, Spread, and Opacity.

Shadows create a sense of depth, which is vital for building a visual hierarchy. In designs with multiple hierarchical levels, keep track of where your objects belong—those closer to the viewer get more attention than objects further away. *Material Design* [11] provides a great example of documenting and explaining its light sources, shadows, and elevation.

11 Light and shadows
https://material.io/design/environment/light-shadows.html

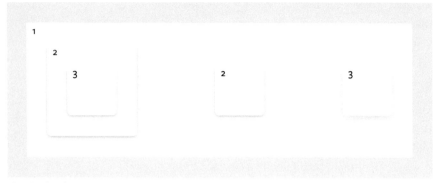

Elevation levels.

Object elevation is especially important in UI controls like buttons, fields, and menus, as their behavior traditionally depends on a sense of depth. Buttons change their depth when pressed, sunken fields invite users to fill them in, and menus pop up on top of everything else.

Shadow *Spread*[12] is important for imitating elevation and represents the distance by which to expand or contract a shadow in all directions. The implementation of this property in Figma is based on CSS property box-shadow, and shares some of its limitations. Currently, Spread can be added only to rectangles, ellipses, and backgrounds of frames and components.

It feels like a hack, but it may be useful to imitate a border on only one side of the object by using a Shadow with Blur set to 0. This effect can be applied to multiple sides by stacking multiple shadows with different offsets together.

12 Behind the feature: shedding light on shadow spread

https://www.figma.com/blog/behind-the-feature-shadow-spread/

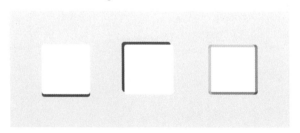

Alternatively, by stacking multiple shadows on top of each other, you can imitate multiple light sources or create incredibly smooth and realistic shadows.

The great plugin *SmoothShadow* provides a lot of control over the result.

Regular shadow vs. SmoothShadow plugin.

Layer Blur makes the layer's geometry look out of focus. **Background Blur** applies the same effect to all the layers under the current layer, but only when it has some transparency. Interface designers can direct the user's attention by blurring some parts of the interface, as humans pay attention to what's in focus and ignore the rest. Apple popularized this effect by introducing translucency[13] in iOS 8.

COPY AND PASTE PROPERTIES

You can copy and paste colors and effects between objects by selecting them in a list and pressing Command-C (Ctrl-C on Windows) to copy, then pasting to another object with Command-V.

13 Translucency and Vibrancy

https://developer.apple.com/design/human-interface-guidelines/macos/visual-design/translucency/

All properties of the object (opacity, fills, strokes, and effects) can be copied from the context menu Copy/Paste → Copy Properties (Option-Command-C or Alt-Ctrl-C) and pasted with Copy/Paste → Paste Properties (Option-Command-V).

SELECTION COLORS

The Selection Colors feature is unique to Figma and lets you view and change colors in multiple objects at once. This is a huge time saver when you are adjusting colors in a group of layers or the whole mockup, as it includes colors in both fills and strokes (but not in the effects [14]). To use it, select multiple layers or a parent object, then review and change colors in the Selection Colors section of Properties panel.

14 https://twitter. com/mwichary/ status/1250129890306711552

By clicking on the target button next to the color, you can select only objects using it, and then selectively adjust them. The Style button with four dots lets you standardize colors within a system, which we'll talk about later.

For situations where you need to be more specific and select all objects sharing the same fill, stroke, or effect, there is a set of features like "Select All with Same Fill/Stroke/Effect/etc." in the Edit menu.

Text

Text is essential for design work, and Figma provides solid tools for working with it. Built-in access to a giant collection of Google Fonts, great alignment controls, advanced OpenType features, selection of useful plugins, and Auto Layout make it possible to create and maintain even very complicated layouts with ease. While occasionally missing things like bulleted lists and placing text on a path, I can see how they may be considered non-critical for an *interface* design tool. I am sure the Figma team will get to them eventually!

Figma works in a browser, and different browsers and operating systems render text differently. It wouldn't be acceptable if the same design looked different based on an environment, so Figma uses a custom text rendering engine. This guarantees a consistent look across all platforms.

To start editing an existing text layer, double-click it, or select and press the Enter or Return key. Once you're in text editing mode, you can edit other text layers by clicking on them once.

CREATING AND RESIZING TEXT BLOCKS

To create a new text layer, select the Text tool from the toolbar, or press the T key on the keyboard. Your next action will determine what kind of a text block you're creating:

- Clicking once creates a text block with resizing set to *Auto Width*. The line of text will be as long as you let it. The new line will be created only if you press the Enter or Return key. This is known as point text and ideal for menu labels, navigation items, button labels, etc.

- Clicking and dragging creates a *Fixed Size* text block. Your text will automatically wrap inside,

but it may overflow the dimensions of a bounding box if it's too long. Normally it's referred
to as area text and used when the area can't be
changed, like in illustrations or overlays.

Don't worry if you changed your mind or picked a
wrong type—it can be changed later in the Resizing
section of the Text panel. There is one more kind of
resizing—*Auto Height* keeps the width of the block
fixed while text wraps and changes height automatically. This works great for paragraphs with longer
copy.

Keep in mind that when you manually resize text
blocks set to Auto Width or Auto Height, their resizing type will be changed as well. Manually setting
the width of the Auto Width block will change it to
Auto Height, while resizing its height will change
it to Fixed Size. Manually setting the height of the
Auto Height block will make it Fixed Size.

Text in Fixed Size blocks can be vertically aligned to
the top, middle, or bottom. This preference doesn't
affect Auto Width or Auto Height blocks.

PICKING TYPEFACES

Let's start by clarifying terminology. *Typeface* is a
collection of characters in a single design, often
including different styles (i.e., italic or oblique) and
weights (i.e., bold or black). It also can be referred to
as a *font family*. On the other hand, *font* is a file with
a set of characters all of one style.

Figma comes with fonts from multiple sources, and
they're unusual because of its browser-based nature:

- **Local fonts** stored on your computer. If you're
  using Figma in the browser, it won't be able to access your local fonts without Figma Font Helper[15]
  app. The desktop app has this functionality built-
  in, so you don't need a separate app.

15 Use Local Fonts with
Figma Font Helper

https://help.figma.com/hc/
en-us/articles/360039956894-
Use-Local-Fonts-with-Figma-
Font-Helper

- **Web fonts** like Google Fonts and Font Awesome. Having them inside a design app is handy if you're designing for the web. Keep in mind that Figma doesn't really integrate with these services, but periodically copies their font files, so font versions can be different [16].

16 https://twitter.com/rsms/
status/1235952641001156608

- **Shared fonts.** This option is available only for users on the Figma Organization Plan [17], but it's worth mentioning. Organization admins can upload and share fonts within the organization or the team, and they will become available to individual users.

17 Upload Fonts to an
Organization

https://help.figma.com/hc/
en-us/articles/360039956774-
Upload-Fonts-to-an-
Organization

If you have an Adobe Creative Suite subscription, you can use Adobe Fonts too, but after activating, they won't become available until you reload the file. To do that, right-click on an open file tab and select "Reload Tab".

Without previews, a font picker can be hard to use. Figma announced its redesign on Config 2020 [18], but it still wasn't released. In the meantime, try a *Better Font Picker* plugin that tries to solve the same problem. It's limited to showing only fonts installed in your system, but that's better than nothing.

18 New ways to create,
collaborate, and share more
openly

https://www.figma.com/blog/
config-2020-new-feature-
announcements/

If a design file uses a font that's not available on your computer, you will receive a yellow missing font alert next to the font in the Text section and in the toolbar's top-right corner. Keep in mind that this can happen even if you have the font, but its version is different. You can ignore this as long as you don't need to edit affected text layers. To fix the problem, install the fonts on your computer or use a built-in Missing Fonts dialog to replace them.

FONT SIZE, LINE HEIGHT, AND LETTER SPACING

The number of available **Font Styles** depends on the typeface. **Font Weight** of a text block or selection can be changed with shortcuts Option-Command-< and Option-Command-> (Ctrl-Alt-< and Ctrl-Alt->).

Font Size is set in pixels on the right of the Font Style selector.

Line Height (also known as *line spacing*) controls the distance between lines of text in a paragraph. Use shortcuts Option-Shift-< and Option-Shift-> (Alt-Shift-< and Alt-Shift->) to change it for a text block or selection. By default, it's set to Auto and matches line height specified by typeface designer, but it can be changed using either percentage (%) of the font size or pixels (px). For example, given a font size of 18 pixels, line height set to Auto will differ from font to font, but set to 100% will always stay 18 pixels. The way Figma adds space around lines and generally treats text is closer to css specification than traditional design apps. For a deep dive and historical context on this topic, check out the article "Getting to the bottom of line height in Figma"[19] by Marcin Wichary.

19 https://www.figma.com/blog/line-height-changes/

Line height dramatically affects the readability and visual weight of a text block. The general rule of thumb is that wider lines of text need more spacing between them, so the eyes can move from line to line naturally, while shorter lines of text can be set more tightly.

Lorem ipsum dolor sit amet, consectetur adipiscing elit. Cras vel mi nec quam efficitur placerat vitae vitae lectus. Donec diam lectus, consectetur in dapibus vitae, lobortis in lacus. Praesent ultricies dolor vel consectetur aliquam. Etiam pulvinar arcu nisi, in tincidunt metus sagittis sed. Sed sed consequat velit, vel luctus quam. In congue pharetra orci, vitae laoreet urna porttitor eu. Sed ut dapibus ante. Cras id nunc nulla. Sed in bibendum purus. Quisque ultricies turpis a venenatis lacinia. Ut malesuada metus ut massa mattis eleifend. Mauris sodales massa eu velit iaculis fringilla.

Lorem ipsum dolor sit amet, consectetur adipiscing elit. Cras vel mi nec quam efficitur placerat vitae vitae lectus. Donec diam lectus, consectetur in dapibus vitae, lobortis in lacus. Praesent ultricies dolor vel consectetur aliquam. Etiam pulvinar arcu nisi, in tincidunt metus sagittis sed. Sed sed consequat velit, vel luctus quam. In congue pharetra orci, vitae laoreet urna porttitor eu. Sed ut dapibus ante. Cras id nunc nulla. Sed in bibendum purus. Quisque ultricies turpis a venenatis lacinia. Ut malesuada metus ut massa mattis eleifend. Mauris sodales massa eu velit iaculis fringilla.

Letter Spacing defines the spacing between characters and can be adjusted with keyboard shortcuts Option-< and Option-> (Alt-< and Alt->). It can be set for the entire text block or tweak the spacing only for an individual letter. Because of the later, Letter Spacing can be used to set *kerning* between individual letters. Having a single control for both settings may not be convenient, but it's good to have a manual kerning option when working on logotypes and more graphical representations of text.

keming

MARCUS AURELIUS

kerning

MARCUS AURELIUS

Spacing between lowercase letters rarely needs to be changed. When text is set in all capital letters, the spacing becomes too tight as capital letters are designed to appear at the beginning of the word next to lowercase letters [20]. Try adding 5–12% extra letter spacing to text in all caps, particularly at smaller sizes.

20 Butterick's Practical Typography: Letterspacing https://practicaltypography.com/letterspacing.html

SCALING TEXT

The previous section covered scaling text in a traditional way, but sometimes you may need to scale multiple text layers at once or have more granular visual feedback during the process. That's when Scale Tool (k) from the toolbar comes in handy—you can select multiple layers and proportionally scale them to the right size. Keep in mind that scaling results in fractional font sizes, which you may want to round up later.

PARAGRAPHS

Paragraph Spacing sets the distance between paragraphs in pixels, usually in a range from a half to one font size. It's a much nicer alternative to an extra line break, which is too big and often wrongly used for this purpose.

In the "Type Details" popup, hiding under ... icon, **Paragraph Indent** provides a way to signal the start of a new paragraph by indenting its first line. Normally it's set to 1–4 times the font size, depending on how wide the text block is.

Matthew Butterick, in his book "Butterick's Practical Typography" [21], nicely explains the relationship between paragraph spacing and indent:

21 practicaltypography.com

> First-line indents and space between paragraphs have the same relationship as belts and suspenders. You only need one to get

the job done. Using both is a mistake. If you use a first-line indent on a paragraph, don't use space between. And vice versa.

Text Alignment options are shown both in standard Text panel and Type Details popup, but the Justified option is available only in the normally hidden pop-up—and for a good reason! Figma doesn't support text hyphenation, and without it, the justified text creates large gaps between words and should be avoided.

TEXT DECORATIONS

Text Decorations like Underline and Strikethrough are not part of the typeface design and generally available in any font. Selected text can be underlined by pressing a standard keyboard shortcut Command-U (just like Command-B universally works for bold font, and Command-I for italic).

OPENTYPE FEATURES

Some fonts hide beautiful secrets inside them, like small caps, ligatures, different styles of numbers, or even alternative versions of some glyphs. Figma does a great job of making these OpenType features more accessible. A list of options displayed in the Type Details popup depends on a font's included features, and some of them may be grayed out—these are available, but not applicable to selected text. The best way to explore all available options is by practice, so play with Figma's OpenType playground [22], or pick a font with a good number of included features—like the default Roboto, Montserrat, Inter, or Vollkorn—and just experiment.

22 https://www.figma.com/file/I7aquUJskPWwudWatNjfkC/Figma-OpenType-playground

Here are some of the things that you may change:

Letter Case settings are different and rely on what sets of glyphs were included in a font file. While

Letter Case

Case   -   AG ag Ag AG AG

Capital Spacing   -   ✓

standard Uppercase, Lowercase, and Title Case options are available in almost every font, a Small Caps and Forced Small Caps options show up only for fonts that include them. **Capital Spacing** option increases letter spacing in text set in all caps or small caps, just as we discussed in the Letter Spacing section. **Case-Sensitive Forms** realign punctuation and symbols to better match text set in uppercase.

Figma's Title Case capitalizes every word in a text block, which is a universal but very simplistic model. I built a plugin *Proper Title Case* that follows capitalization rules from APA, The Chicago Manual of Style, and modern conventions— check it out if you're working with text.

Numbers can be proportional (each number takes as much space as needed) or monospace (all numbers have the same width, great for aligning in code or tables), uppercase (the most common) and lowercase (blends in with text), or a combination of them. They can be positioned on the same level as text, below it (subscript), or above it (superscript). Some fonts may even include beautiful fraction support or slashed zeros.

Ligatures are almost invisible to an untrained eye and provide nicer glyphs for tricky letter pairs, like "ff", "fi", "fl", "tt", etc. **Rare Ligatures** are usually more decorative and less common.

Contextual Alternatives may turn combinations of characters into specific glyphs and symbols based on their surroundings, like arrows in programming fonts or more appropriate ending glyphs in scripts.

Ordinals replaces default alphabetic glyphs with the corresponding ordinal forms for use after numbers. This also enables a numero character №, which is technically a ligature.

Stylistic Alternatives and **Stylistic Sets** were designed to lend more visual interest to type compositions by bringing alternative glyphs and ligatures.

This list is far from being complete and includes only the most common features. If you're interested in learning more about OpenType features in Figma, consider reading "An ode to OpenType: Fall in love with the secret world of fonts"[23] by Marcin Wichary, or reviewing all registered OpenType features at Microsoft Typography[24].

23 https://www.figma.com/blog/opentype-font-features/

24 https://docs.microsoft.com/en-us/typography/opentype/spec/featurelist

USING ICON FONTS

Font Awesome[25] is a very popular and large collection of vector icons and social logos, and it's included in Figma's fonts. Use their cheatsheet[26] to pick an icon or brand, copy it to the clipboard, and paste in Figma. Make sure that font is set to "Font Awesome 5 Free" or "Font Awesome 5 Brands", and pick one of two font styles — Regular or Solid.

25 https://fontawesome.com

26 https://fontawesome.com/cheatsheet

CONVERT TEXT TO VECTOR PATHS

In some cases, you may want to convert editable text into vector paths — if it will be tweaked in a logotype or exported for places where the current font file will not be available. That can be done by picking either Flatten (Command-E) or Outline Stroke (Shift-Command-E) from the context menu. They act differently only when applied to more than one layer at the same time — Outline Stroke will preserve individual layers, while Flatten will combine them into one.

Keep in mind that this command is not reversible, so it's a good idea to duplicate (Command-D) and hide (Shift-Command-H) editable text layers just in case.

PLUGINS

There are a few plugins that improve different aspects of working with text.

- *Typographer*—my plugin for formatting text with typographic features traditionally used in fine printing, like en- and em-dashes, curly quotes, etc.

- *Spellchecker* and *Spelll* use different services to find and correct spelling errors. The former is free, while the latter requires a subscription.

- At the beginning of this chapter, I mentioned that sometimes I miss an ability to place text on a path. Well, plugins to the rescue! *To Path* puts any object or text on a path, and *Arc* curves text upward, downward, or into a circle.

By the way, you can assign keyboard shortcuts to the plugins that you use often. There is no built-in way to achieve this, but if you use a desktop app on Mac, you can do this on the system level:

1. Go to System Preferences → Keyboard → Shortcuts.

2. Select App Shortcuts in the left panel.

3. Click a plus button and pick Figma in Application dropdown.

4. Enter plugin name in Menu Title exactly as it appears in Plugins menu

5. Pick a shortcut and click Add.

When finished, you should see a shortcut next to the plugin name in the Plugins menu. If it doesn't work, most likely there is a conflict with another shortcut in Figma, some other app, or operating system—try picking a new one. As this is a system-wide solution, it can be applied to any other menu item and not just plugins.

Exports

Let's start by talking about pixels and units of measurement. In Figma, one "pixel" actually refers to one "display point". You may be familiar with this concept from *reference pixels* in CSS, *device-independent pixels* on Android, and *points* on iOS [27].

A standard-resolution display has a 1:1 pixel density (or @1x), where one pixel is equal to one point. First retina screens by Apple (like iPhone 4 and MacBook Pro Retina) had a pixel density of 2:1 (or @2x). iPhone 11 Pro has a pixel density of 3:1 (or @3x), where its $1,125 \times 2,436$ device pixels get scaled to 375×812 points. Thanks to this concept, the same websites and apps can be used on different devices without becoming three times smaller on a high-resolution 3:1 screen. Because Figma uses display points internally, even while referring to them as "pixels" for simplicity, it can export assets with different scaling for standard-resolution and high-resolution screens.

Officially, Figma doesn't support print units, but it can export assets not only for screens. Need to print a 3″ ×3″ image at 300 dpi? 3″ ×300 dots per inch is 900, so scale your image to 900 ×900 pixels. At 600 dpi, it should be scaled to 1,800 ×1,800 pixels. Of course, lack of CMYK support is a completely different issue.

Exports in multiple formats and sizes can be set up for any object in the Export section of the Properties panel. Add exports by clicking on the plus icon in the top right corner. Clicking on the minus icon removes the topmost export, which may not be the one you want to delete. Instead, I prefer to select an individual export by clicking on its left side and pressing the Delete key.

Figma supports exporting in PNG, JPG, SVG, and PDF formats. While the first three are popular choices

27 Extra reading:

Absolute Lengths (CSS3 Spec)

https://www.w3.org/TR/css3-values/#reference-pixel

Device-independent pixel

https://en.wikipedia.org/wiki/Device-independent_pixel

Image Size and Resolution (Apple)

https://developer.apple.com/design/human-interface-guidelines/ios/icons-and-images/image-size-and-resolution/

for development, PDF can also be used for exporting shareable and printable documents[28]. The name of the exported file is based on the object name and an optional suffix. If you've used a slash ("/") in the object name, Figma will interpret it as a group and place exported files in a folder according to the hierarchy.

The **Size** of exported raster images (PNG and JPG) can be changed by selecting one of the default values or entering a custom one. Use the letter x to define a multiplier, w to set the width, or h to set the height of an exported image. Clicking on the "Export Settings" icon with three dots reveals an option to export "Contents Only", which will include only selected layer or children of a group or frame. SVG may have a few more export settings discussed below.

Sometimes you may be exporting a file just to pass it to another design app or a text editor. In that case, you may avoid the export step and just copy PNG or SVG to the clipboard in the context menu Copy/Paste → Copy as PNG/SVG.

28 Our path to creating a precise PDF Exporter

https://www.figma.com/blog/our-path-to-creating-the-highest-quality-pdf-exporter/

SVG

Scalable Vector Graphics (SVG) is an open XML format. Unlike other image formats, SVGs can be edited as text, scripted, animated, scaled, and it's widely supported in browsers. When exporting as SVG, an object is not just rendered into an image, but translated into a markup language. This approach has its limitations as not all Figma features are supported by SVG and not all SVG features are supported by browsers.

Figma features that are not supported in SVG:

- Angular and Diamond gradients will be exported as Radial.
- Background Blurs won't be exported.

- Some strokes will be converted to fills.

There are also some extra settings available for SVG exports:

- **Include "id" Attribute**—adds an id attribute based on object names to SVG elements. You need this only when referencing SVG elements from code, so keep it disabled to reduce file size.

- **Outline Text**—by default, all text layers will be converted to vector shapes. Disable it to keep the text editable in other apps, but remember that the font you selected may not be available, and overall rendering may be different on other computers.

- **Simplify Stroke**—available only when you're exporting a Vector Network with an Inside or Outside stroke. SVG as a format only supports Center stroke, so by default, all other stroke types will be converted to it. This may result in an unexpected look, so by choosing not to simplify stroke, Figma will attempt to reproduce the desired outcome with masks and extra code.

SLICE TOOL (S)

The Slice Tool lets you specify a region of the screen for exporting. Its boundaries are independent of the content and may contain multiple objects or only part of an object. When working with the file, Slices stay completely out of the way and can be selected only in the Layers panel.

You can export all Slices and objects with defined exports at once by selecting File → Export in the menu. There, you can see previews, names, formats, and dimensions, and enable or disable individual exports. This is a great way to update all assets defined in your file with a single click.

Creating Layouts

Individual elements, shapes, and text layers can get you far into the design process, but without organizing them into logical and editable units, it will be hard to keep going. I like the way Brad Frost thinks about design organization in his Atomic Design[1] methodology:

1 https://bradfrost.com/blog/post/atomic-web-design/

> Lately I've been more interested in what our interfaces are comprised of and how we can construct design systems in a more methodical way. In searching for inspiration and parallels, I kept coming back to chemistry. The thought is that all matter (whether solid, liquid, gas, simple, complex, etc) is comprised of atoms. Those atomic units bond together to form molecules, which in turn combine into more complex organisms to ultimately create all matter in our universe. Similarly, interfaces are made up of smaller components. This means we can break entire interfaces down into fundamental building blocks and work up from there.

According to this approach, individual layers are *atoms*. We combine them into groups or frames, which are *molecules* of the design—an icon consisting of multiple shapes or a button made of a rectangle and a text layer. These smallest units form *organisms*, such as a website header or a search form. Finally, we put together organisms into layouts of individual *screens*, that can be organized into *pages*.

Figma provides tools for organizing elements on every level of this approach. Thanks to powerful features like Constraints and Auto Layout, we can reuse the same modules in multiple sizes and with different content. Understanding how these tools work will form a foundation for creating reusable components in the next section.

Tidying Up and Smart Selection

Before we get to molecules in the form of groups or frames, let's see what we can do with arrangements of individual layers. Smart Selection makes it easy to reorder or change the spacing between multiple objects. There are only two requirements:

- Objects must overlap on an axis.

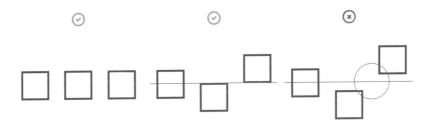

- Spacing between objects must be equal on every axis.

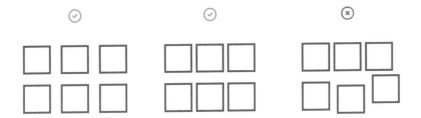

Objects can be of different shapes and sizes, as long as they are aligned and spaced properly.

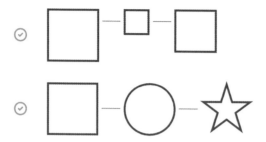

It's easy to align objects on the same axis by using the alignment tools or pressing Control-Command-Arrow Up/Down/Left/Right shortcut.

Inconsistent spacing between objects can be fixed manually, but a better use of your time would be to automatically distribute spacing or tidy up the whole selection.

DISTRIBUTE SPACING

Select a row or column of objects and click the last icon in the alignment row.

In it, pick an option to distribute spacing along their axis. Spacing in a column should be distributed vertically and in a row horizontally. The objects will be spaced evenly between the first and the last ones, which are never moved.

Before   After

TIDY UP

An even smarter *Tidy up* tool lets you automatically redistribute objects based on your selection. Select multiple siblings that you want to set an equal distance apart, hover the cursor over the selection, and you'll see one of the variants of the icon in the bottom right corner.

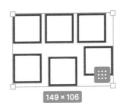

Alternatively, pick *Tidy up* from the same dropdown as Distribute tools or use a shortcut Control-Option-T on Mac or Ctrl-Alt-T on Windows.

Tidying up horizontally or vertically will just Distribute objects, automatically picking a mode based on your selection. Acting on a grid-like two-dimensional selection is more tricky. Figma will do its best to set a consistent horizontal spacing between columns and vertical spacing between rows, but unlike Distribute tools, it may reposition objects on edges of your selection to form a grid.

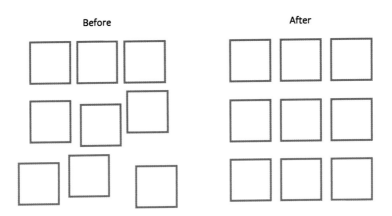

SMART SELECTION

Evenly spaced objects form a foundation for a Smart Selection. When a selection passes the requirements, Figma will show Smart Handles as pink rings at the center of each object. By clicking on them, you can easily rearrange objects in the selection.

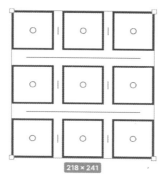

You can resize one or multiple objects in the selection while keeping spacing between them consistent. Select all objects and click a pink ring Smart Handle on the object you want to resize, with Shift if there are a few of them. When an object has a pink bounding box, you can resize it vertically or horizontally while all other objects will be repositioned automatically. You can delete (Delete or Backspace) or duplicate (Command-D) selected objects as well.

When you hover over the Smart Selection, additional handles will show up as pink lines between rows and columns. By dragging them, you can change the distance between rows and columns. (Hold down Shift to adjust in the increments of 10 or your *Big Nudge* value.) You can also set horizontal and vertical spacing in the Properties panel.

Space distribution, Tidying up, and Smart Selection are really powerful tools. You can start with a large selection of disorganized objects and set consistent spacing and arrangement in only a few clicks. Even if you're used to doing all of this manually in other design apps, the saved time is worth forming new habits.

Groups and Frames

Both groups and frames let you combine layers so they can be handled as a single object. That's where their similarities end.

Layer **groups** and folders were part of the design tools for a long time. Their only function is to combine related layers for moving around or organizing purposes. I like to think of groups in Figma as shortcuts to selecting multiple layers with one click. They don't have any properties of their own, their size reflects the children's dimensions, and if you apply fill or stroke to the group, it will be passed to all the nested layers individually.

As the focus of design tools evolved from illustrations to interfaces, the requirements changed as well. Unlike in static illustrations, parts of the interface must be flexible and adaptable to different screen sizes, number of items, and length of copy. To address this, Figma came up with another abstraction in the form of **frames**, which behave as adaptive parent containers with their own sizes, properties, and features.

Frames and groups can be converted to each other at any moment, using a dropdown in the Properties panel.

GROUPS

To create a group, select at least one layer and either choose "Group Selection" in the context menu or press Command-G (Ctrl-G on Windows). To ungroup, select the group and choose "Ungroup" or press Shift-Command-G (Shift-Ctrl-G on Windows). Layers, groups, and frames can be added or removed from the group by dragging them in or out within the Layers panel.

A single click on a group selects the group, and a double-click selects a nested object. If you have a group nested inside a group, it will be selected by a double-click, so you need to double-click again to go one level deeper and select a nested layer. In complex layouts, this can be tiresome, so instead, you can select an individual layer inside any group by holding down a Command key. Another trick is to right-click on an object while holding down a Command key to see all of its parents and children. Of course, you can also select an individual layer in the Layers panel.

Use groups when size isn't constrained, and all objects must resize as a whole. Icons and illustrations are good examples.

FRAMES

Frames are adaptive containers with dimensions defined by the user. As real containers, they have their own properties like corner radius, fill, stroke, and even effects.

Frames can be nested inside other frames, and their level of depth affects their behavior. Top-level frames placed on the canvas are used for defining areas for the individual screens or pages, so they are similar to Artboards in other design tools. Their names show up on the canvas, and they can be used in prototypes or presentations.

Name of the top-level frame

Frames can be created either empty or from selected layers. To create an empty frame, choose the Frame Tool (F) in the toolbar and either drag out an area of the screen or pick one of the predefined popular sizes in the Properties panel on the right. To create

a frame from existing layers, select at least one of
them and either choose "Frame Selection" in the
context menu or press Option-Command-G (Alt-
Ctrl-G on Windows). "Ungrouping" a frame works
the same as for groups.

The frame size can be changed by dragging its
bounding box or editing width and height values in
the Properties panel. It also can be resized to match
the size of nested objects by clicking **"Resize to
Fit"** icon (Option-Shift-Command-R) in the top right
corner of the Properties panel. When the frame is
resized, nested objects move or scale based on the
Constraints set by the user—we will talk about
them in the next chapter.

Frames can be selected in the Layers panel, or if they
are top-level, by clicking on their name on the canvas. Nested objects get selected by a single click, so
save your double-clicks for groups and editing mode.

For maximum efficiency, frames, groups, and layers
can be navigated using keyboard shortcuts. With
a frame or group selected, press Enter to select all
nested objects. Press Shift-Enter to select the current
object's parent frame or group. Use Tab or Shift-Tab
to navigate to the next or previous object accordingly. Esc always clears the selection.

Unlike with groups, objects can be dragged into and
out of the frame. This is only possible because the
frame's size is strictly defined. While dragging an
object, you can hold Command (Ctrl on Windows) to
force an object to nest inside a frame. To prevent an
object from being nested in or moved out of a frame,
hold the Space bar while dragging. This is not an
obvious feature, but without the Space bar dragging
layers around can be surprisingly annoying.

Because nested objects can be partially or completely outside of frame's dimensions, you can choose to
"Clip content" of the frame in the Properties panel.

All the parts "overflowing" frame's boundaries will be hidden. Consider it a built-in clipping mask, matching dimensions of the frame.

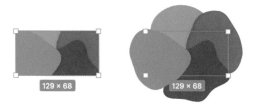

Use frames to create layouts where nested objects should maintain a specific size and location. For example, the navigation on the left and search on the right side of the header, preserved in their size and space when the header is resized from portrait to landscape orientation.

The same frame in two sizes.

Constraints

This is where the fun begins! Until this moment, it might not have been clear why to bother using frames for anything except top-level artboards if groups are so familiar and straightforward. But because the size of the frames is predefined, Figma can be smart about moving and scaling its children.

Constraints define how objects respond when their frame is resized. They help when the design is adjusted to multiple screen sizes, or an element is being reused in different parts of the UI. Constraints can be applied along both the horizontal and vertical axis. By default, they are set to Left and Top, which can be surprising when you resize a frame for the first time.

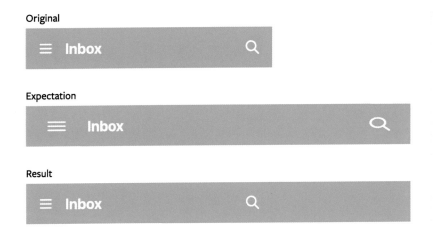

Not at all what you'd expect after resizing groups in the past! Let's see available Constraints for a horizontal axis:

- **Left** maintains the position of the object relative to the left side of the frame and doesn't change size.

- **Right** maintains the position of the object relative to the right side of the frame and doesn't change size.

- **Left & Right** maintains the position of the object relative to both sides of the frame, which will cause it to grow or shrink horizontally when the frame is resized.

- **Center** maintains the object's position relative to the center of the frame and doesn't change size.

- **Scale** maintains the position and size of the object proportionally to the frame's dimensions. It's consistent with how groups are being resized.

Options for a vertical axis work the same, so let's not stop on them. Here is an example of the same frame resized to the same size, but with different pairs of Constraints applied to the children.

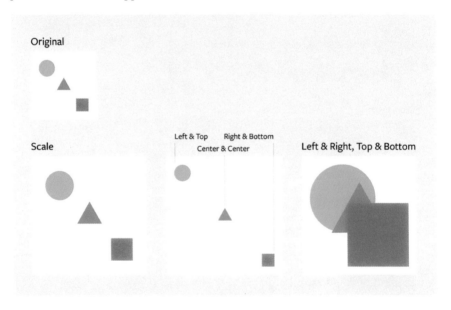

Constraints can be applied to objects or frames nested within other frames. That said, they can't be applied to groups since they always inherit properties from their children and don't have any properties of their own. When an object within a frame is selected, blue dotted lines show which constraints are currently applied to it.

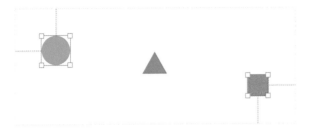

You may need to ignore constraints and resize the frame without moving or scaling its children in some cases. This can be done by holding down Command (or Ctrl on Windows) while resizing the frame. I often use this feature to change the height of the screen to fit the content.

Let's see how Constraints can be used in practice by designing a simple email app screen that can be used both portrait and landscape orientations.

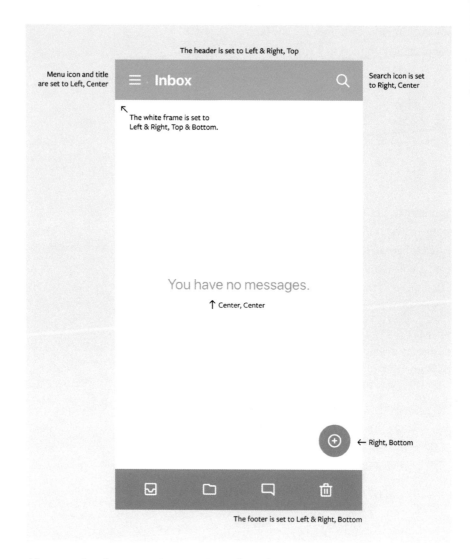

The header is set to Left & Right, Top

Menu icon and title are set to Left, Center

Inbox

Search icon is set to Right, Center

The white frame is set to Left & Right, Top & Bottom.

You have no messages.

↑ Center, Center

← Right, Bottom

The footer is set to Left & Right, Bottom

After creating the screen in portrait mode and setting up all the Constraints, I just duplicated it (Command-D) and changed the orientation to landscape—all objects moved and resized on their own, according to their Constraints.

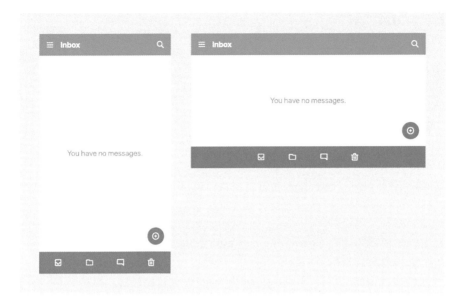

The only area that can be improved is the toolbar at the bottom. It would be nice if icons were evenly distributed across the toolbar instead of being stuck in the center. To achieve this, let's look at Layout Grids.

Layout Grid

Swiss graphic designers started experimenting with grids in the middle of the last century. Over time, grids became a standard way to design structured pages. Considering the role they play in creating consistent, modular, and reusable layouts, it's not surprising that web and UI designers started using them as soon as technology allowed.

At first, grids on the screen replicated paper layouts with fixed dimensions. In 2009, Ethan Marcotte published the article "Fluid Grids"[2] in A List Apart, where he proposed a new way to create fluid grids that resize with the browser window. That was an important milestone in web design, but possible only in code—design tools were lagging behind, still operating in fixed dimensions. Luckily, today this is not a case anymore.

2 https://alistapart.com/article/fluidgrids/

Figma has three tools for creating layout grids—Grid, Columns, and Rows. After adding a grid, click its icon to change type and settings. Layout grids can be combined in any way, even with multiple grids of the same type overlaying one another.

Layout grids can be applied only to Frames. Considering how frames can be nested inside each other, we can create truly modular grids on different levels—columns for the whole screen, rows for a text baseline, a mix of the two for the units, a uniform grid for an icon, etc.

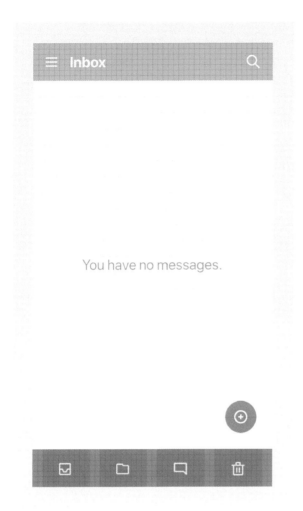

Grid is the simplest one and overlays the frame with a uniform grid of predefined size. It's often used for designing consistent symbols and icons, but can help with screen layouts as well.

By default, the uniform grid size is set to 10px, although 8px grids are much more common. Google's Material Design[3] recommends aligning the overall layout to an 8px grid and smaller elements like icons and type to 4px grid. Check out the article "The 8-Point Grid"[4] for implementation details.

3 Understanding layout

https://material.io/design/
layout/understanding-layout.
html

4 The 8-Point Grid

https://spec.fm/specifics/8-
pt-grid

If you decide to use an 8px grid, consider also changing the "Big Nudge" value from 10 to 8. Big nudge defines the increment of value change with the Shift key held down. It can be set in Preferences → Nudge Amount under the hamburger button.

Columns and **Rows** are more powerful, and can be created either fixed or stretchy.

Fixed columns and rows have fixed width or height and can be aligned to either side or center of the frame. **Gutter** is the space between the rows and columns, and **Offset** defines the distance from the side of the frame where the grid starts (applies only to Left/Right and Top/Bottom). In fixed grids, Count set to Auto will fill all available space with pre-defined columns and rows. Fixed columns and rows are useful if your frame has a fixed size or you're designing for a single screen size, which is rare now.

Stretchy layout grids have almost the same properties as fixed, but their width or height is automatically calculated based on dimensions of the frame, count of columns and rows, gutter, and margin. In stretchy grids, **Margin** replaces Offset and defines the distance between the outermost edges of the layout grid and the frame. Stretchy columns and rows provide a great foundation for responsive design on the web and adaptive layouts in apps.

If columns and rows in alternating colors are too visually heavy, there is a cool trick letting you create lightweight 1-pixel grids by setting Gutter to 0. This is especially nice when you need to show a baseline grid for setting text or to indicating padding inside a frame.

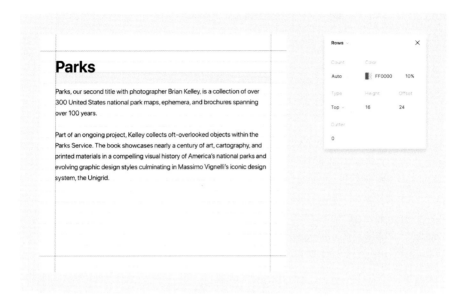

Layout grids are great for aligning elements, but having them visible at all times will interrupt the design process. Individual grids can be hidden in the Layout Grid panel, but most often, I find it useful to toggle all grids visible at the moment. In the top-right corner of the screen, click a Zoom percentage and either enable or disable Layout Grids in the dropdown menu (Control-G on Mac or Ctrl-Shift-4 on Windows).

You can copy and paste grids between elements. To do this, select one or multiple (with Shift pressed) grids on a frame and copy them to the clipboard (Command-C on Mac or Ctrl-C on Windows). Switch to the frame you want to apply a Layout Grid to and paste them using keyboard shortcut Command-V on Mac or Ctrl-V on Windows. A Layout Grid can also be saved to and reused from Styles, but we'll talk about that in the next section.

LAYOUT GRID AND CONSTRAINTS

Using a Layout Grid and Constraints together is one of Figma's lesser-known features, most likely because there is no visual indication of the connection in the app UI. This feature can be discovered only by accident or from reading documentation.

A Layout Grid is not just a visual aid. When applied to the frame, it helps Figma align nested objects when the frame is being resized. If you use stretchy grids, an object's Constraints will be based on the nearest column or row of the grid instead of the frame. This helps maintain fixed gutters and results in more realistic scaling behavior.

Let's return to our email app example, and apply a Layout Grid with Columns to the toolbar.

Icons are aligned to the columns, and their Constraints are set to Center and Center. When we change app orientation to the landscape now, they're properly distributed on the toolbar.

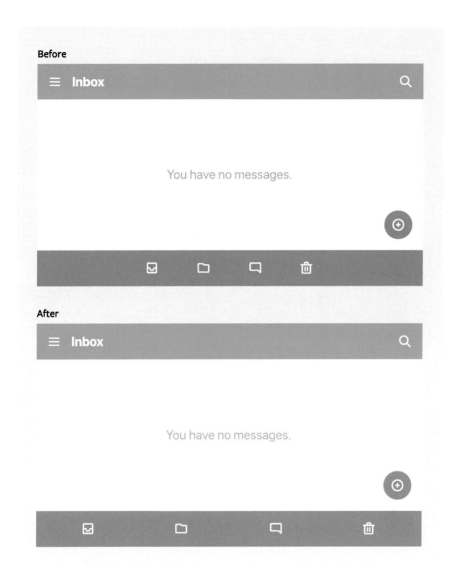

Before & After applying a Layout Grid.

The same technique can be used for maintaining
fixed gutters and margins when resizing the frame.

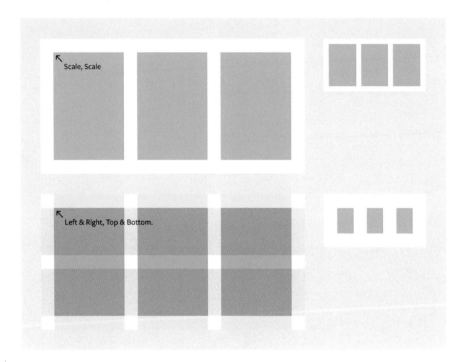

Scale, Scale

Left & Right, Top & Bottom.

In the top example, a Layout Grid wasn't used, and both horizontal and vertical Constraints on the green blocks were set to Scale. When the parent frame is resized, both gutters and margins are scaled proportionally. On the bottom example, a Layout Grid was defined with stretchy columns and grids, and green blocks' constraints were set to Left-Right and Top-Bottom. When resized, all objects stick to the grid.

Rulers and Guides

Rulers and Guides are indispensable when you need to precisely position objects in the design.

First, you need to turn Rulers on by clicking on the Zoom percentage in the top-right corner of the screen and enabling them in the menu. Alternatively, use a quick Shift-R keyboard shortcut.

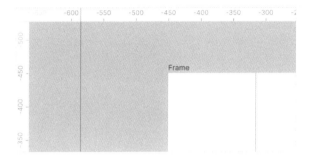

With rulers visible on the top and left side of the canvas, you can create a new guide by clicking on the ruler and pulling it out to the desired place. Figma can place guides either on the canvas to help organize individual artboards, or inside top-level frames. When placed inside a frame, guides will be attached to it even when you move the frame around the canvas. Guides can be deleted either by dragging them out of the screen, or single-clicking on them (the guide will turn blue) and pressing Delete on the keyboard.

Guides are extremely valuable to developers, but they can't be exported to the project documentation. Luckily, there is a nice plugin *Redlines*, that can be used for annotating design mockups during the handoff process. It can outline objects and measure dimensions while providing full control over the look of redline elements.

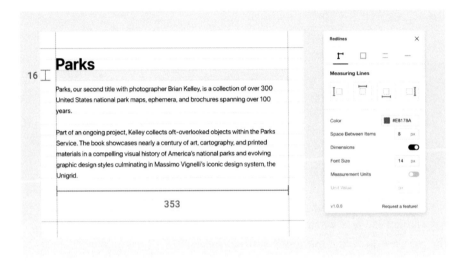

Auto Layout

Auto Layout makes frames responsive to their content. By defining how children are laid out in a frame, Auto Layout dynamically updates the frame whenever content or the number of children is changed. Buttons can grow or shrink with their text, menus can resize when new items are added, and lists can be easily rearranged. It was released only at the end of 2019, but has already redefined how teams design and organize their components.

If you're familiar with web development and CSS, Auto Layout is based on a concept of the Flexbox layout. That shared foundation makes it easier to translate design mockups to real interfaces on the web.

ADDING AUTO LAYOUT

Auto Layout can be applied only to frames. If you apply it to a group, it will be converted to a frame. When applied to a selection of objects, a new parent frame with Auto Layout will be created.

To add Auto Layout, make a selection and click the plus icon in a section of the Properties panel. Alternatively, use keyboard shortcut Shift-A or a context menu item "Add Auto Layout".

Auto Layout   +

It's worth noting that Auto Layout can be added to an object even when the option is not present in the Properties panel. The best example is building a re-sizable button—create a text layer, add Auto Layout with a shortcut or through the context menu, and then style a newly created parent frame.

Auto Layout can be removed by clicking on the minus icon in the same panel, or selecting "Remove Auto Layout" in the menu (Option-Shift-A). Keep in mind that after Auto Layout rearranged objects, their original place can't be restored.

PROPERTIES OF AN AUTO LAYOUT FRAME

Because frames with Auto Layout respond to their content, some of the normal frame properties won't be available anymore:

- Width and height can't be set manually. Depending on the resizing mode, either one or both of the properties will be set automatically.

- Constraints that stretch or change the frame's dimensions (Left & Right, Top & Bottom, and Scale) can't be selected.

- Layout Grid can't be applied.

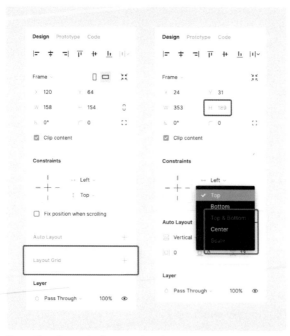

Properties of a regular frame vs. Auto Layout.

Now, let's look at Auto Layout properties of the parent frame.

Direction defines which way the frame will be resized when children are changed or added. *Horizontal* is great for creating buttons with editable text labels or rows of icons. *Vertical* is a good fit for lists or menus. If you apply Auto Layout to existing objects, the direction will be set automatically based on their flow.

Currently Figma supports only one direction at a time. If you need to create a grid-like structure, Auto Layout frames can be nested inside one another.

Resizing controls whether you can adjust a frame's size on the axis opposing the direction. The height of frames with horizontal Auto Layout and the width of frames with vertical Auto Layout can be fixed or set automatically.

Automatic resizing sets the dimensions of the frame based on its content. As you add children of different sizes, they will be laid out in the chosen direction, and the frame will be resized to accommodate them. Your frame will be as big as its biggest child. With *Fixed* resizing, frame's width (for Vertical) or height (for Horizontal) can be set in the Properties panel, and children will be distributed within a frame, possibly even overflowing it.

Padding controls horizontal and vertical whitespace around the children of the frame. At this time, controlling individual sides or negative values (that might be used for overlapping) are not supported.

Spacing Between sets the distance between individual children. Thanks to a combination of Padding and Space Between, you can control spacing on all sides of your Auto Layout children.

PROPERTIES OF AUTO LAYOUT CHILDREN

Because Auto Layout arranges children automatically, some of their properties can't be set manually anymore:

- Position (X and Y) is set automatically.
- Constraints aren't available. Use order and alignment instead.
- Smart Selection isn't available.

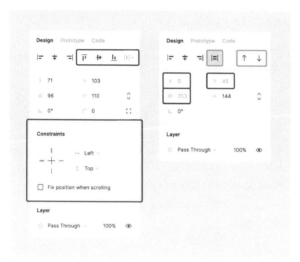

Properties of a regular object vs. Auto Layout child.

Alignment options for Auto Layout children are limited compared to regular objects. They can be aligned only along the axis opposing the direction of Auto Layout. In a frame with the Horizontal Auto Layout, children can be aligned to the top, center, bottom, or stretched from top to bottom of the frame. In a frame with the Vertical Auto Layout, they can be aligned to the left, center, right, or stretched from left to right.

You can shuffle through alignment options with the arrow keys. In Horizontal layout, use the Up and Down keys to change alignment between Top, Center, and Bottom, or hold Option to skip Center and toggle between Top and Bottom only. In Vertical layout, use Left and Right to toggle between horizontal alignment options.

Unlike in regular objects, alignment of Auto Layout children is persistent — once you set the child to be aligned to the side of the frame, it will stick to it even when resized or rearranged. In a way, it acts more like a Constraint than a normal alignment tool.

You can quickly change **Order** of elements by moving the child with arrows in the Properties panel or on the keyboard. Use Left and Right in Horizontal layout, Up and Down in Vertical; Hold the Option key to move the object to the beginning or the end. Changing their order in Auto Layout will also update the order in the Layers panel, and vice versa.

Another way to change both Alignment and Order is by dragging an object inside a frame.

It's worth noting that as Auto Layout frames can be nested, the same frame can be both a parent and a child simultaneously. In that case, both sets of properties will be available, except stretching from side to side. While regular children of an Auto Layout frame can be stretched, a child with its own Auto Layout must resize only in response to its content. Stretching it would be against the core principle of how Auto Layout works.

Why Layers Appear in Reverse Order Inside Auto Layout Frames?

There has been some confusion about why layers appear in reverse order inside an Auto Layout frame. Figma's Director of Product Sho Kuwamoto explained their thought process in a Twitter thread[5] shortly after launch. I'll summarize it to clarify the situation, but I encourage you to read the original for additional details.

5 https://twitter. com/skuwamoto/ status/1204261358428012545

First, let's consider normal layers. When you duplicate a layer, the new one goes above the old one so you can see it. The order of layers in the panel reflects their Z-axis, so the new layer will be above the old one there as well. That behavior is standard for all design tools.

Auto Layout introduced a connection between visual order of objects and order of their layers in the Layers panel. The first object (left/top) is always on the bottom of the layers list, and the last object (right/bottom) is on the top. This is consistent with traditional layers' behavior, but misleading when you consider that the Western world is reading and counting from left to right, top to bottom. If you have an Auto Layout frame with an ordered list 1–2–3, its layers will be ordered 3–2–1.

Sho Kuwamoto shared some ideas on how this can be fixed in his thread. Ultimately, their team decided to keep things traditional and familiar, but they might consider adding a preference to change this in the future.

Using Text Layers in Auto Layout

Using text blocks inside Auto Layout is worth discussing separately. As you may remember, text blocks have three resizing modes—Fixed Size, Auto Width (height is fixed), and Auto Height (width is fixed). There are many parallels between these resizing modes and frames with and without Auto Layout.

Pay attention to what text mode you use inside an Auto Layout frame. Your button won't grow or shrink to match its label if the text is set to Fixed Size or Auto Height. A bullet list made with vertical Auto Layout won't resize its child to fit an extra line of text if the text object is set to Auto Width.

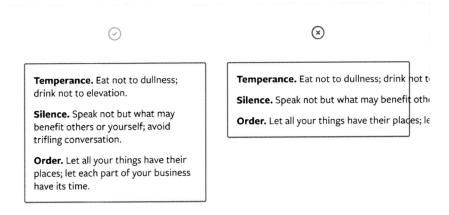

Auto Height vs. Auto Width text inside a vertical Auto Layout frame.

If you imagine that characters and words are individual objects, text blocks can be considered a version of Auto Layout frames. Both regular frames and Fixed Size text blocks can be resized only manually. Frames with Vertical Auto Layout and Auto Height text blocks have a fixed width, but their height depends on the content. The same is true for fixed height and fluid width of a Horizontal Auto Layout and Auto Width text block. Parallels like this may not be intrinsically practical, but they help understand the connection between the tools.

Irregular Spacing Between Components

Consistent spacing between items may not work for every design. In the example on the left, spacing is set to 16 pixels, but the resulting gap between the title and first paragraph is too large. On the right, spacing is set to zero, but instead, I added custom spacer components in two sizes—8 pixels after the title, and 16 pixels around the image. At any moment, I can hide spacers by setting the component's opacity to zero and enjoy all the benefits of Auto Layout with the flexibility of custom spacing. If you decide to go this route, I recommend creating a set of components sized according to a consistent scale.

Using spacers with Auto Layout.

ADDING, REMOVING, AND HIDING CHILDREN

You can add new objects to a frame with Auto Layout by dragging them in. A blue line will indicate the location and alignment of the object inside a frame. Figma will not let you drag in an object larger than a parent frame, but that behavior can be overwritten by pressing the Command key (Ctrl on Windows).

Alternatively, you can duplicate existing children by selecting Edit → Duplicate in the menu or pressing Command-D (Ctrl-D).

Objects can be removed from an Auto Layout frame by dragging them out or selecting and pressing the Delete or Backspace key.

Hiding an object will make it disappear and change the order and move all other children. That can be done by clicking on an eye icon next to layer's name or pressing Command-Shift-H. This is a powerful way to create reusable components with multiple states, but we'll get to that soon. If you need to hide a child but keep a gap in its place (as in a spacer example above), set layer's opacity to zero.

Pages

Pages provide a way to organize individual screens and components inside a file. Specific ways to use (or not use) pages are up to you and your team, but here are some ideas:

- Keep previous iterations or rejected versions on a separate page.
- Dedicate one page to your design system and components.
- "Experiments" page, so your team won't comment on unfinished work.
- Organize larger projects by feature or section.

Naming conventions are highly individual. Personally, I like to name pages starting with emoji to make them easier to scan.

The need to use pages depends on the complexity of your project. For smaller projects, keeping everything on a single canvas can make things clearer and easier to manage. It's easy to add pages and rearrange a project once it gets to the point when extra complexity is justified. Objects can be moved between pages using the "Move to Page" command in the context menu. You can use shortcuts Fn-Arrow Up and Fn-Arrow Down to navigate between pages.

Let's see how large teams use pages to organize their files and projects.

Dropbox splits their design system libraries into pages for layout, typography, OS-specific icons, components, and in some cases, fully-composed screens:[6]

6 Design Tooling at Scale
https://dropbox.design/article/design-tooling-at-scale

> The component pages in these kits are the most utilized portion of our library ecosystem and are organized into quickly-scannable sticker sheets. The organization of

these sheets is important — in recent internal user testing, we discovered that about
half of Dropbox product designers prefer to
copy and paste directly from these sheets,
rather than using Figma's Assets panel in
their files.

Component pages from Dropbox Web library.
Image by Adam Noffsinger © Dropbox

Spotify wrote an extensive post[7] on organizing work
inside Figma. They use a single spec file per product
that represents a single source of truth, and inside it
use pages for all of the features:

7 How Spotify Organises
Work in Figma to Improve
Collaboration

https://spotify.design/article/
how-spotify-organises-
work-in-figma-to-improve-
collaboration

"Where's the latest design?" is a message
we send and receive far too often. Similar
to how we're bringing visibility to explora-
tion work through our new Team and Project structures, we also wanted to pull specs
out from individual files and into the open.
Each Team (i.e. product) now has a single
spec file, and within those files are pages
that represent each of our features. As a
designer hones in on a solution, they move
their work into these centralized specs to
document their decisions.

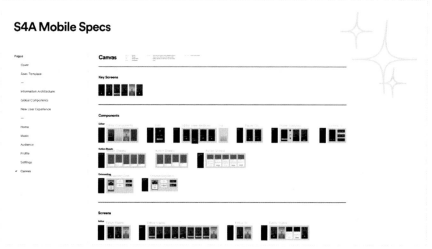

Feature page in a Spotify spec file.
© Spotify

Hosts of *Design Details* podcast Brian Lovin (GitHub)
and Marshall Bock (YouTube) discussed their approaches to Figma organization and handoff process
in episode "Versioning and Handoff in Figma"[8].

Brian uses a new file for every version of GitHub's
mobile app, and inside them creates an individual
page for every new feature and improvement that
will be a part of that release. That way, the team has
a dedicated file for every sprint, and every page contains a discrete change that will be shipped.

Marshall creates a line to separate pages that are
final from pages that are exploratory. That indicates
to the team that these pages are work in progress
and shouldn't be shipped. He likes to use emoji to
indicate the status of the pages as well, for instance,
🚢 for ready to be shipped or 🔍 for explorations and
experiments.

Ultimately, it all comes down to communication and
conventions within your team. It's easy enough to
experiment with different approaches, and over time
you'll settle on a system that works for you and your
team.

8 Episode 340: Versioning
and Handoff in Figma
https://designdetails.fm/
episodes/318485

CUSTOM FILE THUMBNAIL

By default, the first page of the file is shown as a thumbnail in the file browser. When there are multiple screens or artboards on the first page, everything becomes tiny, and the thumbnail gets hard to scan. The problem is even worse when your project has multiple files with similar content. Luckily, the team at Figma thought about this and provided a way to define custom file thumbnails.

On any page, create a new frame with dimensions 1920 × 960. The thumbnails' width in the file browser is changing based on the window size, but the center 1600 pixels of the thumbnail is the safe zone that will always be visible. After designing a clear and easy-to-scan thumbnail, right-click on a frame and select "Set as Thumbnail" in the context menu. The frame will get a special icon, and the file's thumbnail will be updated.

File thumbnail.

Thumbnails in the File Browser.

To remove a custom thumbnail, right-click on the frame and select "Restore Default Thumbnail" from the context menu.

Consider designing a custom template for your thumbnails and adding it to the Team Library. It may include things specific to your needs, like a status of the design (finished or live, in progress, archived), ticket number, or the iteration's version. This way, your whole team will be on the same page and can avoid contributing to or implementing the wrong version of the file.

Links

Links provide a new way to navigate within Figma. They can point to individual frames, pages, files, and projects within Figma, or even to external resources. With links, you can create navigation within a file or collect all relevant docs and resources for a larger project in one place.

The Link can be added to an entire text layer or a selection of text within the layer. Linking other objects is not supported at this moment.

To add a link, select text or a text layer and click the "Create Link" icon in the toolbar. Alternatively, use Command-K (Ctrl-K) keyboard shortcut. If a URL is already in the clipboard, you can even skip the dialog and just paste it (Command-V) to create a link.

Links to individual frames and pages can be copied in their context menu. Link to a file can be copied either from Share dialog when it's open or from its context menu when you're inside a project. Even the whole project can be linked by copying a link from its Share button.

Building
a Design System

So far, we discussed creating basic elements and organizing them into flexible modules and layouts. Only one piece of the puzzle is left untouched—figuring out how to reuse these modules, layouts, and properties of the elements across the whole project.

In this section, we'll talk about creating reusable components and sharing properties as styles. Components, in particular, are very flexible, so we'll go through different approaches to build and organize them. Then, we'll look at building a Team Library from components and styles that can be used across all your files and projects. This will provide all the building blocks for creating a solid design system shared by the whole team.

In the book "Design Systems"[1], Alla Kholmatova writes about establishing a design system in the organization:

> How does a team start thinking about design more systematically? Typically, when they notice issues with their current workflow. Designers become frustrated always solving the same problems, or not being able to implement their designs properly. Developers are tired of custom styling every component and dealing with a messy codebase. Both struggle to meet the deadlines and demands of a growing product. Without shared design language and practices, collaboration is difficult.

The way these tools are built and how I think of them is heavily influenced by software engineering. You don't need to know how to code to use them, but getting familiar with the tools and concepts used by developers will help you speak the same language. Bridging the gap between design and development is good for everyone, but the real winners are users who end up with a more coherent and well-built product.

1 Meet "Design Systems", A New Smashing Book
https://www.smashingmagazine.com/design-systems-book/

Components

Components are objects that can be reused across the project. They let you split the design into independent, reusable pieces to ensure consistency and maintainability.

Design apps had the concept of *symbols* for a long time. At first, they were reusable objects that couldn't really be customized. Things started to change when React gained popularity for building interfaces around 2014. It introduced designers with front-end skills to component-based development, which gave them full control over the presentation and behavior of individual components. Coming back to primitive symbols in design apps was painful, and so from 2014 to 2016, all major apps stepped up their game.

Figma was still very young when it added *components*, which helped avoid many mistakes and limitations of other apps. Even the name of the feature suggests a transition from tools of the past to modern design and development practices. Figma Principal Designer Rasmus Andersson said it nicely while introducing components [2]:

2 Components in Figma
https://www.figma.com/blog/components-in-figma/

> As someone who comes from a background in both design and engineering, I've noticed the way we design is very different than the way we build software. People expect complex user interfaces that are alive, connected and always improving. How can we keep up as designers? Engineers have already figured this out.

Components in Figma are based on frames, but duplicating them creates new *instances* rather than disconnected copies. Changes to the original main component translate to all instances, which can have their own overrides. Just as frames, components can be nested to form complex modules from individual pieces. That's a quick summary of how components work, but now let's look at them more closely.

MAIN COMPONENTS AND INSTANCES

Components can be created from any layers, groups, or frames. Internally, they are based on frames, so if you turn one into a component, all its properties will be preserved. Creating a component from a group will convert it to a frame, and collections of objects will be wrapped in one.

To create a component, make a selection and click icon *Create Component* in the toolbar, or press Option-Command-K on the keyboard. You can also select the command from a context menu.

That creates a **Main Component** (in the past known as *Master*), which defines the properties of the component. It has a quadruple diamond icon, and its name is shown in bold in the Layers panel. All main components also appear in the Assets panel. You can quickly switch between Layers and Assets panels using Option-1 and Option-2 shortcuts.

❖ Main Component

An **Instance** is a linked copy of the component that inherits its properties. Any change made to the main component will also apply to all its instances. To create an instance, use one of the ways:

- Duplicate the main component (Command-D or drag with Option/Alt).
- Drag instance out of the Assets panel.
- Copy and paste within one file.

Instances have a diamond icon, and their name is shown in regular font. The purple color sets main components and instances apart from regular objects, both in the Layers panel and in their bounding boxes.

◇ Instance

You can quickly return to the main component from an instance by clicking on the "Go to Main Component" icon in the Properties panel.

By default, main components remain in the place where they were created. This makes it easy to see and tweak them in the context of your design, but may be unusual if you're coming from Sketch where symbols have a dedicated page. (See *Component Page* plugin if you miss that.) Larger projects also benefit from having a dedicated page or file with the whole design system in one place. As a rule of thumb, I move components to a separate place only when I need to use them on more than one screen. Until then, I keep them in place to simplify editing and reduce overhead.

NAMING AND ORGANIZATION

As your projects grow, so will the number of components. It's important to have a consistent structure to keep them organized. Ultimately, your team should come up with naming and organizational conventions and then follow them rigorously. Looking for components in an unorganized mess is a good way to waste time rebuilding duplicates.

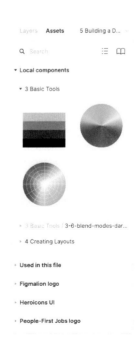

In the Assets panel, components are grouped by their source and path. For now, we will focus on *Local components* and get to components from Team Libraries in another chapter. The path to a component will follow a general structure of File / Page / Frame / Component Name.

Pages will be displayed alphabetically and ignore their manual sorting order. If you have only one page in a file, it won't be a part of the structure.

Components created inside a **frame** will show its name in the path. That's handy if you keep some main components on the screens they belong to, or group related components together (i.e., "UI controls" frame to keep all the standard form controls together on a dedicated page). Avoid keeping common components in random frames — it will be hard to remember that the Button component is inside the Dashboard frame.

Component name can contain slashes to group related components. For instance, if you have a set of icons, you can name your components "Icon / Add", "Icon / Remove", and "Icon / Like" to keep them all together.

In the Component section of the Properties panel, you can write a description of the component. It will be displayed as a tooltip when you hover over it in the Assets and Inspect tabs, but more importantly, it will be indexed by search. This is a great place to add alternative names, so you can find your "Like" icon by keywords "heart", "love", or "favorite". The search field is available on top of the Assets panel.

Aside from keeping the Assets panel organized, your structure and name grouping help Figma determine **Related Components**. To be considered related, components must be arranged within the same frame or be a part of the same name group. In this example, all the logos used in the project will be shown as Related Components.

While we're on this, it's worth noting that Figma supports renaming multiple layers, groups, or frames at once. Select them and either pick Rename in the context menu, or press the Command-R keyboard shortcut to open a dialog. You can change multiple layers to the same name, add a prefix or a suffix to existing layers' names, or add numeration. By using the *Match* field, you can update only a part of the name. This is especially handy if you want to rename a group name in multiple layers, i.e., change "Banners/…" to "Ads/…". The Rename form even supports Regular Expressions, if you're familiar with using them.

SWAP INSTANCES

Components can be easily **swapped** in three different ways—by finding a replacement in the Instance menu, by dragging a component from the Assets panel, or by using the context menu. This is a great way to quickly switch between icons, UI controls, and other related components.

The Instance menu is the easiest way to swap components. It provides quick access to related components but also lets you navigate to other hierarchies and groups, search for components, and even switch between libraries.

You may also drag a component from the Assets panel and drop it above the instance you want to swap while holding the modifier key. If the component isn't nested within another frame or component, hold the Option (Alt) modifier key, otherwise use Option-Command (Alt-Control on Windows).

Finally, the most limited but often the fastest option is to use the context menu. Right-click on the instance and select one of the related components in the "Swap Instance" menu.

OVERRIDES

Overrides let you change properties of an instance to use the same component in more than one way. They play a big role in making Figma components more powerful than a previous generation of symbols in other design apps. Here are some examples of using overrides:

- Button component used with different text labels. Build it with Auto Layout, and every instance will auto-resize to its text label size.

- Applying custom color to an icon component.

- Changing a photo in an avatar component.

- Form with different states of the controls and values of the fields.

Not all properties of an instance can be changed, or it would lose any resemblance and connection to the main component. You can change these properties:

- Size of the instance

- Text content and styles

- Fill, Stroke, and Effects

- Visibility and opacity of nested layers

- Swap nested components

Some properties can't be overridden:

- Size or position of nested layers

- Layer order

- Constraints

- Layout Grids

You can see and reset all overrides applied to the instance or a nested layer from the "Instance options" menu in the Properties panel.

What happens when you override some properties of an instance, but then swap it with another instance? Figma will attempt to preserve your changes, but layer names and hierarchy need to match between the current instance and the instance you're selecting.

Sometimes you'll make changes to an instance and then realize that the whole component should be updated. You can push changes from an instance back to the main components by using the "Push Overrides to Main Component" command from the "Instance options" menu in the Properties panel. That will also update all other instances of that component. "Push Overrides to Main Component" is supported only when main component is in the same file as an instance.

DETACHING INSTANCES

When you need to change an Instance beyond supported overrides, it's time to Detach it from the component. That will turn it into a regular Frame and remove the connection between it and the main component. The instance can be detached using the "Detach Instance" command in the "Instance options" dropdown menu in the Properties panel, a context menu, or shortcut Option-Command-B (Ctrl-B on Windows).

Be careful! Every time you detach an instance, you end up with a disconnected frame with some properties of the original component. Consider building your more complex components by combining simpler swappable components. This way, it'll be easier to customize an instance without detaching it from the main component. Generally, consider detaching instances a "code smell"[3] of the project—a characteristic that *possibly* indicates a deeper problem. On an Organization plan, Figma can even track how often instances are detached with Design System Analytics to suggest when components aren't flexible enough.

3 Code smell
https://en.wikipedia.org/wiki/Code_smell

If you no longer need a component, but want to keep its objects in place, it can be deleted by detaching. Create an instance of the component and detach it, then delete an original main component. The component will disappear from the Assets panel.

If there were other instances of the deleted main component, they would end up with a broken link to the main component. In that case, you can either detach them as well, or use the "Restore Main Component" command in the instance section of the Properties panel.

PRINCIPLE OF SINGLE RESPONSIBILITY

As we established before, components borrow a lot from software engineering. It's not surprising then that principles used by software engineers for decades can now be applied to the design of the components. One of them, *the principle of single-responsibility*[4], states that every component should be responsible for a single part of software functionality and that responsibility should be entirely encapsulated by it.

This principle is a little harder to apply to design components than to programming functions, but we can try. If you're familiar with programming, I like to think of components as functions and overrides as arguments (or props in React). When we're adding an override, we're not changing the component itself, but just calling the function with a different set of arguments. Let's look at the example.

4 Single-responsibility principle

https://en.wikipedia.org/wiki/Single-responsibility_principle

The header component for Postmark.

This header is built from smaller components. We can present its structure as a nested list.

- Header
  - Logo
  - Navigation
    - Nav Link / Default
    - Nav Link / Default
    - Nav Link / Default
    - Nav Link / Active
  - Subnav Bar

- Subnav Items
  - Subnav Link with Icon / Active
    - Icon / Message Streams
    - Text label
  - Subnav Link with Icon / Default
    - Icon / Templates
    - Text label
  - Subnav Link with Icon / Default
    - Icon / API Tokens
    - Text label
  - Subnav Link with Icon / Default
    - Icon / Settings
    - Text label

Header component can be changed only to reorganize how *Logo* and *Navigation* are laid out on a yellow bar. *Navigation* is responsible for a number of *Nav Links* and spacing between them, but not their content or presentation.

Subnav Link with Icon / Default is responsible only for the layout of an icon and text. The *Active* version reuses it, overriding color and adding a border at the bottom. I can edit text, but the component defines its style, or I can swap the icon component, but its content is not a concern of the *Subnav Link with Icon*.

Because every component is responsible only for its own thing, I can change the style of a *Text Label*, and it will be applied both to *Default* and *Active* states of the *Subnav Link with Icon*. I can change the spacing in *Navigation* by tweaking its Auto Layout, and that won't affect its content on any of the mockups. It may feel like you're doing extra work by abstracting smaller pieces of the UI, but it will be worth it as soon as your project gets slightly bigger.

INHERITANCE

Inheritance is another important principle in software engineering, and I briefly touched on it in a previous section. Consider these two components.

They are constructed from two nested components, *Icon* and *Text Label*. How can we maintain consistent spacing and layout between *Default* and *Active* versions of the component? If we build them independently, eventually they will get out of sync.

We want an *Active* state to inherit *Default* layout and spacing, and then apply its own styles on top of it. That can be achieved by creating an instance of the *Default* component, changing its colors with overrides, adding a border on the bottom, and then wrapping it all into a new component for an active state.

With this approach, we'll follow both single responsibility and inheritance principles—*Active* component will be responsible only for an active style because it inherits *Default*, which is responsible only for layout. Win-win!

VISIBILITY OVERRIDES

Some components may have a large number of versions. Consider tweets.

In addition to a text, they may include a link thumbnail, image, audio, video, or even another tweet. If that wasn't enough, there could be "♥ Username liked" or "Promoted" badges on top and bottom as well. How do you manage all these cases?

The common approach is to create a main component that includes all the modules, and then **use layers visibility overrides to create an instance for every version**. This is where Auto Layout shines, as it treats hidden elements as removed from the flow and rearranges all children of the frame. In the end, create new components for the instance versions to easily reuse them in the future, i.e., *Tweet / Quote Tweet, Tweet / Liked Tweet, Tweet / Promoted Link*, etc.

If later you'll need to adjust the size of the avatar or change the font of the username, it all can be done in the single main component. This approach is nicely based on two principles we just discussed.

VARIANTS

There is a better way to organize related components than just grouping them by name. *Variants* let you combine components sharing the same properties but with different combinations of values into a single component set. Image if you could switch between variants of the previous tweet component just by setting values of its properties.

Common examples of variants include buttons, inputs, notifications, navigation menus, and any other sets where all components are not completely unique but built on a shared foundation. That said, not every group of components has to be turned into variants. Figma doesn't recommend using variants to group different icons, although they can be used to combine different sizes of the same icon.

Variants simplify the Assets panel by significantly reducing the number of components and map design components more closely to components in code. For example, buttons in design systems will usually have separate components for every type, size, and state, while in code, they will be implemented as a single Button component accepting different properties. Talk to developers to ensure that your choice of language and properties is consistent between design and codebase.

Component sets can be one- or multi-dimensional. The one-dimensional component set has a single property with two or more values (e.g., Button with Default, Hover, Pressed, and Disabled states), while the multi-dimensional set has multiple properties with different options available for each property (e.g., Primary and Secondary Button, each available in several states, with or without icons).

Multi-dimensional component set

Combining existing components with shared properties into variants is pretty straightforward:

1. Review component names. When related components are grouped using forward slashes in their names, the first group will be interpreted as the name of the component set. Each next group is treated as a new property with values populated from names at that level. For example, components *Button / Primary / Default, Button / Primary / Hover,* and *Button / Secondary / Default* will become a component set *Button* with two untitled properties with values *Primary / Secondary* and *Default / Hover*. (You can organize and rename them later, but it's easier to start with a solid foundation.)

2. Organize components into one- or multi-dimensional structure on canvas. Consider adding labels outside of the component set for future reference. The top left component will be used as a default variant and represent the entire set in the Assets panel.

3. Select the components and click the "Combine as Variants" button in the sidebar. Notice that all selected components turned into variants of the component set and now have a single diamond icon.

4. Figma automatically creates variant properties from name groups and populates their values based on names, but it doesn't know the names of the properties. It will name the first property *Variant*, then number them sequentially: *Property 2*, *Property 3*, and so on. Rename property names in the Variants panel.

5. Binary values like *On/Off*, *True/False*, *With Something/Without Something*, etc. can be represented as toggle switches. Use True and False or On and Off for such values.

6. Properties can be reordered by dragging a handle appearing on hover to the left of the property name.

It's also possible to create new variants from scratch, although the experience is a little bit more cumbersome:

1. Start with creating a component.

2. Click the "Add New Variant" button in the Properties panel.

3. Name the value and change the default property name.

4. If you're creating a multi-dimensional component set, add more properties by selecting "Add New Property" in the "More Options" dropdown in the Variants section.

5. Add values by selecting a variant inside a component set and either entering a new value or clicking "Add new..." in the property dropdown.

Now when you turned individual components into a component set with variants, it can be used as any other component. The main practical difference is that the component set can't be duplicated or copy-pasted to create an instance, so drag it from the Assets panel.

CREATING COMPONENTS IN BULK

If you ever import a large collection of icons or objects into Figma and need to create components from them, there is a better way than doing this manually one by one. I've done this before. It's not fun. Select multiple objects, and you will notice a dropdown arrow appear next to "Create Component" button in the toolbar.

Click an arrow and select "Create Multiple Components", so Figma can create a component from each object you selected. This is not something you'll use often, but it will save a lot of time when you do.

VERSIONING COMPONENTS

If you're working on a project for a long time, you'll eventually need to redesign one of the components from scratch. Alternatively, you may import a project from Sketch, and automatic conversion of symbols into components won't use any of the powerful tools Figma has to offer. **What to do when you can't just update an existing component, and it's already used across the project?**

In a situation like this, I'll create a new version of the component and manually replace old instances with the new ones. The overwrites will be lost, but sometimes it's faster to copy-paste data than try to migrate everything. Here are some tips on making this process easier:

- Create a new page "● Deprecated" and move deprecated main components to it.

- To draw attention to deprecated instances, cover the main component with a bright half-transparent layer.

- Use *Instance Finder* plugin to find all instances of the deprecated component.

- After doing a large cleanup or migration, it's worth running *Unused Components* to see if any of the components can be removed.

- In a large project with hundreds of screens, it's not realistic to update all instances at once. This may be fine, as long as your team can easily tell that the component is deprecated and knows where to find a replacement.

Creating a new version of the component is also useful if you want to explore different design directions. Just remember to clean them up when you settle on the best one.

Styles

Components and styles are like yin and yang of the design system—one is responsible for content and functionality, while another is all about appearance. Styles allow you to define and reuse a set of properties across the project:

- Color Styles (including solid colors, gradients, and images)
- Text Styles
- Effect Styles
- Layout Grid Styles

Once defined, styles can be reused and changed globally across the whole project. It's a great way to make design consistent and uniform.

CREATING STYLES

Styles for different properties can be created and managed in the same way. Select an object with a solid color, fill, effect, text style, or grid you want to reuse as a style. Inside the Properties panel section, click the Style icon with four dots to open the Styles dropdown.

In the dropdown, click the plus icon to create a style. Styles created in the current file will be shown on the top. Just like components, style names can contain slashes to group related styles. For instance, you can have multiple headers organized like "Headers / H1", "Headers / H2", etc.

One of the popular approaches is to pick names that communicate roles or functions of styles rather than just describing them. There are certain benefits to organizing styles this way. For example, if the design has a specific accent color, it's much harder to accidentally pick its wrong shade when Color Style is clearly named "Accent". It's also more meaningful and future-proof—the color itself may eventually change, but the name will stay the same.

While this approach works great for Text Styles, it may be tricky to follow for colors on a larger project with more extensive visual language. On Postmark[5], we have an extensive color palette with numerical names for shades of colors.

5 https://postmarkapp.com

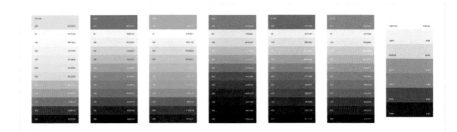

For more ideas on naming conventions, I highly recommend exploring large organizations' design systems in the Figma Community. There are different approaches, and it's best if you settle on what works best for your team and projects.

APPLYING STYLES

To review all styles used in your file, click on the canvas. In the Properties panel, they will be listed in the Local Styles section and organized by type. Notice how icons of Effect Styles reflect positions of the shadows — I love Figma's attention to small details!

That's a good place to review, organize, delete, and modify styles. The order in this list will be reflected when you get to use them, so keep them organized by dragging.

To apply a style to an object, select it and click the Style icon in the Properties panel. Select one of the existing styles in the Styles panel. Later, you can switch between styles the same way.

Local Styles

Text Styles

Ag Figma UI

Ag Figure / Default

Ag Figure / Small

Ag Figure / Tiny

Ag Blend numbers

Color Styles

● Figma UI / Selection

● Good

Light Background

Effect Styles

◡ Testimonial shadow

◡ CTA Bottom

Grid Styles

||| 8 columns

When using a color picker, you may notice that a new group Local Colors appears in a dropdown next to Document Colors. It may look like just another way to apply Color Styles, but it's not. The color value will be used, but the style will not be applied when selected this way. Still, it's a convenient way to create a new color based on an existing Color Style.

MODIFYING STYLES

Changes can be made only to Local Styles of the file. We'll discuss Team Library in the next chapter, but keep this in mind when some styles can't be changed.

To modify a style, select an object using it, open the style dropdown, and click the Edit Style button. Alternatively, switch to the canvas and click the Edit Style button next to a style name in the list.

After you make changes, they will be applied to all the instances of the style in the file.

DETACHING STYLES

Like components, styles can be detached when they need to be modified without affecting all instances. The connection to the style will be lost, and you can freely modify the properties of an object without affecting other instances. To detach a style, select an object and click the broken link icon next to the style name.

Team Library

Most projects will eventually grow out of a single file. We discussed how large teams organize their pages, files, and projects in the chapter on Pages, but here are some common ways to break down a larger project into multiple files:

- A file with project identity and brand colors.
- Separate files for a marketing website and an app.
- One file per platform an app exists on (iOS, Android).
- Key features or sections organized into individual files.
- A new file for every new version of the app.

By default, components and styles are local to the file they were created in. To reuse them across files and projects, you can publish them to the Team Library. This universally available library can help maintain a consistent look and feel across all parts of the project.

Currently, publishing components to a Team Library is available only on paid and educational plans. Publishing Styles is available even on a free Starter plan.

PUBLISH TO THE TEAM LIBRARY

If you already have a file with components and styles that you want to publish to a Team Library, you can do this from the Publish Library modal. It can be opened in two ways:

- Click on the canvas to reset the selection, then click the arrow next to the file name in the toolbar, and select "Publish Styles and Components" from the options.
- Switch to the Assets tab in the Layers panel, then click the "Team Library" icon with the book on

the right (or press Option-3 on Mac or Alt-3 on Windows). Inside the Libraries window, click the "Publish" button next to the current file name.

Inside the Publish Library modal, you can add an optional description that will be saved into Version History, and review a list of styles and components that will be published.

Try not to pollute your Team Library with styles and components specific to just one file. You can choose not to publish any style or component by right-clicking on its name and selecting "Remove from library". It will be marked as "Private to this file", and your choice will be remembered in the future. If you change your mind, right-click on it again and select "Add to library".

While it gets the job done, I find this method of exclusion cumbersome—you have to toggle components one by one, and there is no way to tell if a style or component is part of the Team Library. A better way is to prefix the name with an underscore or a period, and they will be excluded automatically. Choice of the symbols is not accidental. Starting a name with a dot makes a file or a directory hidden on Mac and Unix, and in programming, starting a function name with an underscore is a common way to mark it private.

USING A TEAM LIBRARY

To access a style or component from the Team Library, first you need to enable access to the library that contains it. In the Assets panel, click the Team Library icon, and enable a specific library in the Libraries window. You will see a new group of shared components from that library appear in the Assets panel. They can be used just like any other local components.

The Assets panel organizes components into multiple groups:

- *Local components:* Components that you created in this File. Subgroup "Private to this File" includes components that were excluded from publishing to the Team Library.

- *Used in this File:* Components from other files that you have already used in this file.

- *Enabled Libraries:* Any default libraries that anyone has enabled in a Team or Organization.

Shared styles don't show up next to Local Styles in the Properties panel, which may be a little unexpected. You can access them in the Style panel that is relevant to that specific property, i.e., Color, Text, Effect, or Layout Grid. In there, local styles go first, and every library is separated with a horizontal ruler.

PUBLISH CHANGES

Eventually, you'll need to either change or add new shared components and styles. To avoid accidental changes, publishing changes to the Team Library is a manual process. You'll see a notification in the bottom right corner asking you to publish changes to your Team Library.

Even if you dismiss it, dot indicators next to the Assets tab and the Team Library icon won't let you forget about unpublished changes.

Click the "Publish..." button in the notification or inside the Libraries window, and you'll see the same Publish Library modal that we used for an initial publication of the library. There, you can document your changes and see a list of styles and components that were changed and will be re-published.

Nobody wants their shared components and styles to change in the middle of their work. After publishing changes to the Team Library, every file that uses a shared library will need to manually pull those changes.

ACCEPT UPDATES

When one of the libraries that you are using is changed, you'll see a dot indicator next to the Assets tab and a notification about available updates.

After clicking "Review", you will be presented with all components and styles that were changed. You can update them all at once or individually.

The manual process of publishing and accepting changes may feel excessive, but it keeps your team accountable and avoids unpleasant surprises. You can always review the version history and see who, when, and why made a specific change. This is exactly why software engineers use version control systems like Git to manage codebases instead of relying on automatically synced directories like Dropbox or Google Drive.

REMOVE FROM A LIBRARY

There are situations when you may want to remove a file from a Team Library. Maybe there is a newer version of the design in a different file, or you migrated to a shared design system—you can pull it off at any time.

Go to the file you want to remove from the library and open Team Libraries window from the Assets panel. Click a current file name, then click button "Unpublish" on the bottom of the window. After confirming the action, the file will be removed from your Team Library. All files that use its components and styles will still use them, but won't receive updates in the future.

MOVE COMPONENTS AND STYLES BETWEEN FILES

Organizing your design system with shared styles and core components in a separate file may not be easy if all elements were already created elsewhere. Styles can be moved between files without breaking the connection, but the process is a little backward. Moving components will require plugins and some manual work.

To move a style, start with going to your destination file and enabling a file containing a style in the Team Library. Shared styles aren't shown in the Properties panel, so first, you need to apply a style from the Team Library to an object. After that, click the "Edit Style" icon next to its label.

You can't edit a style shared from another file in place, but you can either "Go to style definition to edit" or "Move style definition into this file". The last option is exactly what we need, but be careful as the style will be moved without any confirmation. "Undo" can't reverse this action, but you can go to an old source file and repeat the process for moving it back. Moving a style won't break the connection, so this process is not destructive.

If you thought moving styles was tricky, wait for components. Unlike styles, main components can't be moved between files. Copying a component from one file to another creates an instance of that component. Your only option is to turn that instance into a new main component, share it in your Team Library, and then manually replace instances of an old main component with the new one in all files. As discussed in the chapter "Versioning Components", you can use *Instance Finder* plugin to speed up that process.

Version History

Version History lets you review and restore earlier versions of a file. Figma automatically saves a new version every time there have been no changes to the file for 30 minutes. This behavior is very useful as is, but we can make it even better by manually saving and naming versions. I mentioned Version History in the chapter on Team Library, but here we'll look at it more closely.

VIEW VERSIONS

There are two ways to show Version History:

- Use menu item File → Show Version History.
- Click on the canvas to reset the selection, then click the arrow next to the file name in the tool-bar, and select "Show Version History" from the options.

Version History will replace the Properties panel on the right and present a list of edits with timestamps and author names. You can click on any version to see a preview. To switch back to the current version, either press Escape or click the "Edit Current Version" button on the toolbar's left side.

SAVE AND NAME VERSIONS

It's hard to stay oriented in a long list of autosaves, and Figma doesn't provide any tools for highlighting the differences between them. To make Version History more practical and useful in the future, we should do extra work today and give versions descriptive names.

You can create a new record in Version History manually without waiting for 30 minutes of inactivity. Either choose "Save to Version History" from the File menu, use a keyboard shortcut Command-Option-S,

or click on the Plus icon inside the Version History panel. You'll be presented with a dialog familiar from publishing changes to the Team Library.

While the dialogs are not exactly the same, both create a new record in history with a unique name and description.

You can add a name and description to any existing autosave by selecting it and clicking on the "More Options" icon with three dots, then choosing "Name This Version". This approach won't let you create granular versions if you worked on multiple things one after another, but it's a good way to organize your existing history.

As we're moving away from "mockup_final _v2_final_v3_final-for-real.psd" file name conventions, it's time to apply the best practices for writing version comments from software engineering to design software:

- Summary in the title, more detailed explanation in the description.
- Write imperative titles: "Fix typo" and not "Fixed typo" or "Fixes typo".
- If you use an issue tracker, reference the issue in the description.
- Use proper capitalization and punctuation.

Randall Munroe summarized the usual progress of writing comments quite well in his xkcd comic.

COMMENT	DATE
CREATED MAIN LOOP & TIMING CONTROL	14 HOURS AGO
ENABLED CONFIG FILE PARSING	9 HOURS AGO
MISC BUGFIXES	5 HOURS AGO
CODE ADDITIONS/EDITS	4 HOURS AGO
MORE CODE	4 HOURS AGO
HERE HAVE CODE	4 HOURS AGO
AAAAAAAA	3 HOURS AGO
ADKFJSLKDFJSDKLFJ	3 HOURS AGO
MY HANDS ARE TYPING WORDS	2 HOURS AGO
HAAAAAAAANDS	2 HOURS AGO

AS A PROJECT DRAGS ON, MY GIT COMMIT MESSAGES GET LESS AND LESS INFORMATIVE.

RESTORING AND DUPLICATING VERSIONS

Figma provides two ways to travel in history. If you hit a wall with a wrong direction or accidentally messed up a file, you can **revert to a previous version** by selecting it in Version History, clicking on the "More Options" icon, and choosing "Restore This Version" from the menu. It's great that this action is non-destructive, so it'll create a new record based on the selected one without erasing your latest changes.

If you want to explore an alternative direction without losing your progress on the current one, you can "Duplicate" a version. Your current file will be left intact, but **an exact copy of the selected version** will be created. It's worth noting that a duplicate won't have the version history, comments, or sharing permissions of the original.

Working With Data

The conversation about Figma won't be complete without discussing the many ways to use real data in designs. Figma provides a powerful API that hundreds of developers use to create great plugins. You can search for them in the Figma Community, while I'll outline some popular choices for a few common use cases. It's hard to keep up with plugin updates, so use their documentation for specific usage instructions.

CONTENT REEL

Content Reel is made by Microsoft for building a library of text strings and images to use in your designs. It comes with a standard library of icons, avatars, and sample strings like names, addresses, and phone numbers, but you can also add your own content. Think of text strings that you use again and again in the mockups, like names of personas, titles of blog posts, descriptions of products, etc.

The best part is that you can use Content Reel to quickly fill your mockups with realistic data. While designing a job board, I created a list of job openings with multiple instances of a job listing component. Then, I defined a new group with job titles in Content Reel, and in one click applied them to a list of instances as text overrides. Later, I reused the same job title strings on other screens.

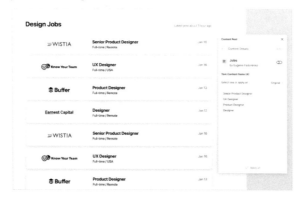

GOOGLE SHEETS SYNC

Decoupling content from design is a great way to
make your mockups more maintainable and enable
collaboration with people who won't be comfortable
using a design app. An unofficial *Google Sheets Sync*
plugin lets you keep all your data in Google Sheets,
name layers using a special convention, and then
sync data from Google Sheets to a Figma file in one
click.

Image by Dave Williames.

This plugin is especially important if you have multiple representations of the same data, like a grid and
list view, desktop and mobile versions of the screen,
etc. By following a simple naming convention, you
can keep a single source of truth for your data and
avoid manual updates.

CHART

Plugin *Chart* uses real or random data to create 16
types of the most popular charts. (Don't confuse it
with a different plugin *Charts*, which only supports
random data and six types of charts.)

Image by Pavel Kuligin.

You can enter tabular data, link Google Sheets, upload a csv, or link a json file as a source of data. It's really powerful and a huge time-saver if you use charts in your designs, but most features require a reasonably priced Pro account.

HTML TO FIGMA

Have you ever needed to iterate on the design of a live website for which design files were long lost or outdated? Before recreating them from scratch, give *HTML to Figma* a try. The first time I ran it, the result was about 80% correct. It's not perfect, but it's easier to clean up an auto-converted mockup than to recreate every asset and element manually.

CUSTOM PLUGINS

Figma's plugins are relatively easy to build, so some companies build internal plugins for their specific needs and use cases. They can be distributed as an archive or a Git repository without making them public in the Community. For example, Microsoft built an internal plugin[1] to switch between color themes of their many products.

1 https://twitter.com/figmadesign/status/1157398695001894912

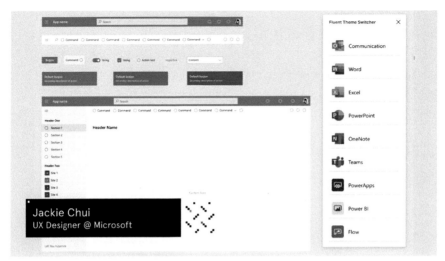

Image by Jackie Chui © Microsoft

Brian Lovin built ten small utility plugins while working on GitHub mobile apps [2], between them color helpers, data population from GitHub API, and dark mode switcher.

2 Automating the Boring Parts of Product Design

https://brianlovin.com/overthought/automating-the-boring-parts-of-product-design

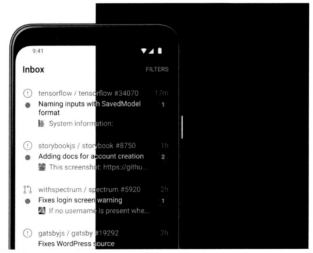

Image by Brian Lovin © GitHub

He presented some of these plugins in a lighting talk at Figma's Config 2020 conference [3], along with demos of other internal plugins by teams from Uber and Atlassian.

3 Extend what's possible with Figma Plugins

https://youtu.be/SyS3h3kmBnY

USING REST API

While plugins let you update designs with data from other sources, Figma's REST API [4] provides a way to read and extract data from Figma as images. Some teams go to a great extent to integrate Figma into their apps, using it as a visual CMS (Content Management System).

Michael McMillan shared on Twitter [5] how his team was tired of manually exporting apartment plans created in Figma to the app they are building, and automated this process with an API:

> At the company I work at (*https://bustbyte. no*) we're building a web app for exploring housing projects to potential buyers. The user can hover over apartments and filter them based on price, square meters and more.
>
> To make hovering work we have to manually outline each apartment, we do this using Figma. This works great, but it's tedious to export each outline (svg path) and import that to the app for every apartment.
>
> Instead of manually syncing outlines between Figma and the app, we use Figma's REST API. Now the app pulls down the outlines in realtime, without 1) manually exporting each outline 2) committing them to git 3) redeploy the app. This is a 10x time saver.
>
> This made us think: What if we used Figma for everything (and not just the outlines): price, sold status, square meters, number of rooms? Essentially turning it into our CMS.
>
> So we did! We use Figma's comment feature to add metadata to each apartment.

4 Figma REST API https://www.figma.com/developers/api

5 https://twitter.com/michaelmcmillan/status/1230795934671548416

This is obviously a hack, but turns out it's really nice! It lets us make changes to the app directly from our image editor. No dev overhead whatsoever.

Check out his thread on Twitter for screenshots and images.

Another example is Mixkit Art, a library of free art and illustrations. The article "How we're using Figma as a CMS for Mixkit Art" [6] shares how their team automated the export of assets:

> When we're ready to publish the new work, we have a Lambda script that connects to the Figma API. We enter an ID and it exports the high resolution assets and copies them to S3, and from there we can then make it live on the site for users!

Building all of these solutions required some time, but only your team can know if it's worth the investment. I think it's great to know that the option to build something with data in your Figma files is always here, patiently waiting.

6 https://medium.com/@mixkit/using-figma-as-a-cms-for-mixkit-art-how-were-using-figma-uniquely-7c8ce30dacc5

Conclusion

When I started looking for a Sketch alternative, at first I didn't take Figma seriously. I realized the huge potential of the app only after spending some time with it. Figma led the way for the next generation of design tools, and new browser-based tools like Framer X and Invision Studio only proved them right.

The strength of Figma is not in powerful components, shareable styles, or presentation tools. These things can be copied or improved by other apps. I believe their core strength is in collaboration, openness and extensibility of the platform, and a vibrant community.

Because Figma is just one click away in the browser, it opened the doors for collaborators who never before participated in the design process. Between product managers commenting on a new screen, copywriters editing text in-place, and developers copying the right color from the Inspect tab, it was never easier to work together.

Openness and extensibility of the platform allow replacing missed functionality with plugins, writing internal plugins to solve problems unique to your team, or even integrating Figma into projects as a source of content. Their team worked hard to make plugin development accessible to anyone with basic knowledge of modern JavaScript.

As of this writing, the Figma Community platform is still in beta and just recently was opened to the public, but the number of contributors and quality of resources is fantastic. I was thoroughly impressed when the day after Apple's WWDC (World Wide Developers Conference) multiple iOS 14 UI kits and widgets were already built and shared for free. I'm looking forward to the future where Figma becomes the GitHub of design, and we can reuse and build on top of each other's work.

This book examined Figma's design tools, provided plugin recommendations, discussed the best practices, and a little bit of design theory. I hope you learned a thing or two—I definitely did while doing the research! If you want to stay up to date with Figma's releases, resources, and news, subscribe to my regular newsletter *Figmalion*. It started as a research project for this book but, over time, became the largest collection of Figma-related resources.

Thanks for reading! I'd love to hear your comments or questions. Send me an email at *hello@efedorenko. com* or reach out on Twitter at *@efedorenko*.

—Eugene

Made in the USA
Coppell, TX
29 November 2023

24954906R10100